KENT

IN THE FIFTIES SERIES

Kent

Reginald Turnor

with wood engravings by
Monica Poole

JOHN HALLEWELL PUBLICATIONS
172 HIGH STREET, ROCHESTER
KENT, ENGLAND

Hop Garden in winter near Capel

First Published 1950 by Paul Elek.
This reprinted edition published
1978

ISBN No 0 905540 16 6

Contents

I

Kentish Outline

SOME say that Kentish Men are descended from Saxons, and Men of Kent from Jutes; others that the distinction is purely geographical, with Men of Kent hailing from east of the Medway, and Kentish Men from west. The division of the county into East and West is thought to be a relic of the eighth century, when the Kingdoms were two ; and such rivalry as has survived is perhaps best expressed by the existence of the Buffs and the Royal West Kent Regiment.

Of widely separated authorities on these differences, the Venerable Bede held the Saxon-versus-Jute theory, and Mr. Richard Church detects a strain of dark wildness and fantasy in the west and south, deriving from some remnant of Celtic blood. Ethnology, however, is far too complicated a science for me to attempt its simplification here.

The inhabitants of Kent might, all the same, consider themselves the most civilised of Englishmen, if only by reason of being the most continental. For, in no state to spread culture anywhere, our semi-barbarous islands drew it always from the south—first from the Romans and later, through the wider diffusion of Christianity, from France. And obviously, Kent was the first part of the country to benefit from these influences.

Mr. Church reminds us of two extremely significant facts : that Kent just managed to escape the ice which covered northern Europe after the end of the Pliocene Age ; and that before the birth of the English Channel between Paleolithic and Neolithic, Kent and Northern France were joined together. He fancies, even, that some prehistoric characteristics may still survive, imaginatively at least, to make Kent the most European English county. The imagination or theory might, of course, also be applied to Cornwall and Brittany, but their history has been altogether different, and distance discouraged the transference of invaders and ideas. It is no insult to Westerners, moreover, to say that everywhere in our country they have been in the rearguard of civilisation; the wilder and hardier natives always retreating westward into the mountains to carry on sporadic warfare, while their more peaceable brothers succumbed to and made terms with the enlightened enemy. For, unlike now, when progress cannot be established by military conquest, those were times when it could be achieved most easily by that means.

Julius Caesar, landing (probably) at Deal, found the inhabitants of Kent already no less civilised than the Gauls; so that even then there must have been a decided superiority of culture over the rest of England. The Romans, with their ports of Regulbium, Rutupiae, Dubrae, and Portus Lemanis (Reculver, Richborough, Dover, and Lympne), seem to have had very little trouble with the natives; setting up their government headquarters in Kent at a time when Thanet was an island.

But for a number of reasons the Romans abandoned England to the Dark Ages—possibly rather less dark in Kent than elsewhere; and in 449 (as has lately been emphasised), the British King Vortigern invited the Jutish brothers, Hengist and Horsa, to help him against the Picts. Fifteen hundred years later this event was celebrated by the arrival at Broadstairs of the modern Danish Vikings rowing their beautiful ship *Hugin*, of which I shall write more later.

Hengist and Horsa were in fact the first of the long series of Dark Age invaders; for of course, having once been given Thanet as a beach-head, they soon took charge of the whole county; and having killed off Horsa, Hengist reigned as King with his son Aesc. The Britons were driven out into the more defensible west.

Coherent history begins only with Aethelbert, great-great-grandson of Hengist, who was King of Kent from about 560 till roughly 616. An evidently progressive monarch, he devised a code of Law and, being married to Berta, the Christian daughter of the Frankish King Charibert, welcomed the mission of St. Augustine in 597. There had already been a Roman Christian settlement in Canterbury, and it was there that Aethelbert, after Augustine's invasion of peace and good will, allowed his monks to settle and preach the Gospel. The King was himself converted; Augustine became the first Archbishop of Canterbury, founding also the sees of London and Rochester; and, after the anti-Christian reign of Eadbald, the new religion was enforced throughout Kent by his son Erconbert.

We cannot claim the site of the Norman landing, but the earldom of Kent was first held by Odo of Bayeux, the Conqueror's brother, and second by William of Ypres, whose tower stands on the higher slopes of the pyramid of Rye. Later earls were Hubert de Burgh and Edmund of Woodstock, younger son of Edward I, before the title passed to the families of Holland, Neville, and Grey. It was raised to a dukedom for Henry Grey, fourth earl, in 1710, and after dying out in 1740, became once more a royal title in 1799. The holder was Edward Augustus, fourth son of George III and father of Queen Victoria.

Religion and defence: the most Christian county, with a great share of its lands belonging to the Church, and the only possessor of two bishoprics; gateway to conquest and first in the battle-line; occupied by Romans and Saxons and defended by four of the

Distant view of Canterbury Cathedral

Cinque Ports against later potential invaders; and, most lately and fatefully of all, main field beneath the skies in which the Battle of Britain was fought—that battle whose loss might well have brought in an age of barbarism more lasting than any Kent and England have known. That is a quick and vague historical flash.

The geological picture is dominated by chalk and clay, North Downs and Weald; with the more recent strata around the Thames and Medway estuaries and the fluctuating Romney Marshlands; and the Upper and Lower Greensand which, enclosing on three sides a large central area of the county, give it its loveliest hills.

The sea, which is the county boundary for a hundred miles, has taken away from and given back to Kent some of its fifteen hundred-odd square miles on the east coast and around the estuaries; so that we have islands like Thanet, Grain, and Oxney, which are no longer islands; ports like Sandwich and Faversham which are no longer ports; and strange transitory islets in the Medway estuary amid desolate marshes and flats.

Our three sizeable rivers—Thames, Medway, and Stour—flow west to east; the two last, with the humbler Darent, making welcome valleys in the Downs. But the Thames, despite Gravesend and the Hoo Peninsula, seems not to belong to Kent—that northern edge is lost to the county in all but fact, clinging by spirit to the world of shipping, industry, and the London purlieus. The Medway and Stour, however, are all our own, and so are the streams of Beult, Teise, and Eden; and Swale makes Sheppey a genuine Kentish Island.

I said the greensand gave Kent its happiest hills. Its Ragstone Ridge is, too, generally higher than the Downs; first cousin to the Surrey Hills and so, of course, without the dry choked chalkiness of the Downs. Trees, hedges, and pasture are the richer, and views more beautiful than any others in Kent. I live on this ridge myself, and so may be prejudiced, but I will admit that it is not Kentish in the sense that the Weald of Cranbrook and Goudhurst, or, I suppose, the great flat cornfields of Thanet, are Kentish. It could be in Surrey. But it is not. For if it is sparing of orchards and hop-gardens, it overlooks them and is the eyrie from which Kent may best be seen.

Orchards and hop-gardens—yes. People think first of fruit and beer when it comes to the word Kent. Next, perhaps, among the well-informed, of bricks and tiles; of small shipyards; of Whitstable oysters possibly; of agriculture naturally, as, still, in most parts of England. But there was once the great forest of Anderida, shared by Hampshire, Sussex, and Kent; denuded by the iron-smelting furnaces before the days of coal. And now there is coal itself. It is mined in the north-east of the county, by Betteshanger and ominously near Canterbury. All I will say now is that it is not at present threatening to create a Black Country of the south.

Paper mills have already a Kentish history, but Crayford and Dartford are beyond the range of rural anxiety, and Plaxtol, one of my favourite villages, seems not to suffer from their branch activities. It is the same with cement, since Gravesend, Chatham, and Rochester must claim interest other than that of the countryman, and Snodland is lost to him. Dartford and Erith one must think of as more London than Kent; industrialised with chemistry, electricity, and transport, though not without some wharfish charm.

My personal picture of Kent is very obvious: cherries and apples; blossom and fruit at their appropriate seasons; hop-gardens and oasthouses. Oasts, indeed, are more typically Kentish than anything else, natural or man-made. They are the county signature or rebus. But there are, too, windmills; some whole, many derelict; and the white-painted weatherboarding of farms, cottages, barns, and mills. And there are cliffs and sands and caves, and the emphatic chalk. Buildings—I shall come to them in a more detailed survey. We have as fine a collection as any county, though none so specially personal as our oasts. We have brick and tile; stone, half-timber, and flint; everything, in fact, which has preceded the threat of universal concrete. And we have that, too.

Writing of any county, one must start with an imaginative picture, however vague; and proceed to detail and clarify it, filling in the broad pattern with historical, topographical, and architectural motifs which are intended to make it graphic and, as it were, mentally portable. I give you, hopefully, my Kent.

Cornfields in Thanet

Shipping on the Thames Estuary, looking to the Essex coast

2

Thames, Darent, and North Downs

IT is best to start from London, for otherwise the temptation is to ignore and disown our connection with it; one cannot end a book on Kent with Bromley and Beckenham, but one can so begin it; and part of Kent is metropolitan, or at least suburban. It is not prosperously and blandly suburban like Surrey where it touches London; but rather industrialised by Thames shipping in the north and speculatively residential in the west; an area where—it is a hard saying not meant unkindly—few people would live for choice.

There is Bromley, which happens to be the town I like least in Kent. It has a long history, and naturally there are a few good things left—the old bishop's Palace, the seventeenth-century college for clergymen's widows, the "White Hart", and what the bombs have left of the fifteenth-century church. And, of course, others. But the whole place is vulgarised by bad building both commercial and domestic; its streets disfigured by shop fronts of chromium and sham marble and hemmed in by ugly building estates. What is good is swamped and insulted by the décor of Woolworth, Odeon, and the Building Societies.

The High Street has lost the house where H. G. Wells was born the son of a cricket pro. and a lady's maid. By reason of his extraordinary breadth of vision and versatility in the field of literature, he is, I think, a Kentish celebrity who can be claimed as a genius. In 1866, when he was born, Bromley must have been a pleasant place, since most of its infelicities are not Victorian but of our own age.

There is Beckenham, more shapelessly unrecognisable as a historic entity; Hayes, where the common still spreads decently above and amidst the indecencies of chaotic building, and where both Pitts lived; Keston, whose common adjoins Hayes', where Romans encamped and, in our time, the control-room of Biggin Hill aerodrome retreated a very little way to an Italianate villa; Chislehurst and Orpington, once real villages but now probably Kent's most select suburbs. Chislehurst claims Sir Edmund Walsingham, Lieutenant of the Tower and official torturer; executioner of More and Fisher, Anne Boleyn and Catherine Howard—to all of whom our hearts go out. His nephew, Sir Francis, Elizabeth's Secretary of State, was rather more respectable, but he worked mainly on a system built on lying, spying, and bribery; and played a great part against Mary Queen of Scots, whom one must always love. I doubt if anyone could love Napoleon III, however, who lived at Chislehurst with the Empress Eugénie after the collapse of the Second Empire. The greater blame may be with Bismarck and the Germans, but Napoleon certainly had done everything possible to make war certain in 1870.

Dartford, taking its name from the Darent, is more industrialised than any town we have yet seen; but it is honest and not vulgar. Wharfs, barges, and cranes, and even, in some lights and positions, tall chimneys, have a pictorial if not an architectural quality. They mean business, too—the necessary business of transport and manufacture. Paper-making and engineering are the main industries, and it seems that they actually began in Dartford—the former in 1607, when the first mill was put up by Sir John Spielman; the latter in 1590 at the first English rolling-mill for iron sheets.

"The river Darent, running under its main street past Gundulph's tower, Trevithick's workshop, and Wat Tyler's cottage, gives Dartford a little harbour before it meanders across three miles of marshes, picks up the Cray, and pours itself into the Thames." So says Arthur Mee's *The King's England* volume on Kent, and says it well. Wat Tyler is possibly our most famous proletarian leader; Trevithick first got the idea of using steam for ships; and Gundulph was the Norman bishop of Rochester in 1077 who began the building of Dartford church as well as his own Cathedral.

Quite a few houses and inns of the eighteenth and early nineteenth centuries give smooth and restful patches in the muddled streets of Dartford. It is a much better town than Bromley and, by the skin of its teeth, maintains its independence from London. But its interest is now largely historical; it is more to be read about in guide books than to be seen; and so has only a small place in an impression such as this.

And Crayford a yet smaller: its present history is of paper and chemicals, but here was the Roman camp Noviomagus; here Hengist beat the Britons to become King of Kent; and here, at Barnehurst, lived our own Sir Cloudesley Shovel. Having risen from gentleman volunteer to admiral, he was wrecked off the Scillies in 1707 and drowned with 800 men. (Some say he was washed ashore alive and murdered for his emerald ring.)

The Crays are different. They retain a stubborn and defiant insistence on being villages which are not in the country; refusing to be anybody's suburbs. They are four—North, St. Mary's, St. Paul's, and Foot's Cray; united by their own little river and linking by road the parent Crayford with Farnborough under the Downs.

As you go north-eastward from the Sevenoaks–Bromley road, your first Cray is St.

Cement Works at Swanscombe

Mary's. There is a desolation of industrial paraphernalia in the fields to the west, and a melancholy range of old weatherboarded cottages butting on the very piers of the viaduct. There is a paper mill and chimney and a long too-narrow street. But it is a village, not an infection; not pretentious or jumped-up like many more complacent neighbours. Students of odd architecture should look at the Temple Congregational church, of flint and stone, with almost unclassifiable columns and towers. It might be Byzantine or Romanesque. Or not. Near it is an excellent Georgian house, at present a W.V.S. centre, which poses no such problem.

St. Paul's Cray, next northward, is another medley of village and industrialism; of cellulose and dungarees; with the Bull Inn and old cottages; and Foot's Cray, though it has rather lost caste and been victimised by suburban tentacles, still has a country lane off the main street. Here you can see "The Old House" and "School Cottages" at the beginning of a narrow, wriggling mile before you come upon a fresh outburst of speculative building. On your right is the still open estate of Foot's Cray Place, a great Georgian house more or less copied from Palladio's Villa Capra at Vicenza. (Two others are known to me—Lord Burlington's Chiswick House, and Colin Campbell's Mereworth Castle in our county. All three greatly inflated Palladio's flat dome.)

Foot's Cray, like Chiswick, has lately been taken over for preservation by a merciful local authority; but since I saw it a fire has done much damage and its future is more doubtful than ever. It was empty and barred to visitors, but in a summer of drought, grass and weeds had kept their place, and the sense I got was hopeful rather than melancholy. In a way, the surrounding vandalism has given Foot's Cray a new charm—or rather an old one belonging to a dream. I don't suppose this dream is peculiar to myself:

you are walking in London and suddenly you discover a countryside of hills and woods within it. You are amazed, elated, a triumphant explorer.

Foot's Cray Place, after the depression of semi-detachment and bungaloid morbidity, gives you something of that sense of discovery. You go through the collapsed entrance gateway, and in the drive lose sight of almost all the encroaching nastiness; and the gardens, planned with a simple and unassuming magnificence, are so placed that only a little planting would remove all offence from the prospect.

The house has four Ionic porticos forming a square round and below the dome; a great flight of steps leads down southward to the first of the lawns; there is the happy Georgian marriage between formality and rurality. It is a small palace, not very well textured in the stone, but orderly, gracious, and reposeful; one more monument to the age of taste and reason. On the main axis, beyond the lawns, trees form a triple avenue spaced with nave and aisles, and there are fields butting on the lane.

You have to go back to a vast main road go-me-round in order to proceed sedately, as it deserves, to North Cray. It is the most villagy of all Crays, and for a short while you can suppose yourself to be in the country. There is not much of it: the entrance to the vanished North Cray Place, and next to that the vast elm by the little church near the Cray; and a few cottages. The church appears to be all Gothic Revival, but inside there is Chantrey's sculpture of Lady Ellenborough, who died aged twenty-six not long after Waterloo. She was the sister of the hated and tragic Castlereagh, who committed suicide at his house, Woollett Hall, near here. The lane takes you through fields and past the avenue and park of Spring Place into Bexley.

It is a wonderful surprise for anyone who goes there for the first time or already knows Bexley Heath. No two places could be less alike. Here is half a mile of real village High Street, with a church set back a little way in a bend. It has one of those extraordinary double spires, of which varieties are at Brookland in Romney Marsh and Upchurch by the Medway estuary. Bexley's is the most uncomfortable-looking of all; an unconvincing alliance of square and octagon; looking as if one extinguisher were trying to extinguish another. But it is interesting by reason of its oddity.

The High Street has, too, the sensible and mellowed Georgian Cray House; a most dignified little group of cottages designed symmetrically with a central pediment; and, opposite them, a really fine weatherboarded mill graced by some of the most wonderful weeping willows I have ever seen.

You soon come upon a by-pass road and are suddenly in the London suburbs, but there is still a lane to be found running east under the Bexley Heath ridge, and the discovery of another little piece of countryside. On the south side of this lane is Hall Place, whose estate, with that of Danson Park, has so happily insulated its mile length. You look through iron gates at something which is so superlatively romantic that you easily believe the story that the Black Prince and the Fair Maid of Kent honeymooned at Hall Place. The site, anyway, is Norman; the house Tudor, with two projecting wings and two great windows such as you find—but only one—in most halls of the period. It is all in softly weathered chequer-board grey: patterned in lacy and cobwebby stone. And the gardens are beautiful.

Danson Park has been made into a museum, and in the grounds are a swimming pool and a lake for boats. It was once the home of the seventeenth-century John Styleman, who married five wives, one of whom was wife to three husbands. It is to be hoped he had a good memory.

All this cannot last, and Crayford soon dismisses romantic ruminations. But above the lane, Bexley Heath has the unusual virtue of southern views over apparently unsullied country, seen from a long and traffic-congested street. There are some decent houses of the early nineteenth century which look rather shabby and disillusioned, but on the whole the place is an ordinary collection of chaotic building of the suburban sort.

The lie of the land here is, however, very much more interesting than where the northern London tentacles suck. From this ridge, even now, you can look over the Cray Valley to the Downs, and William Morris must have chosen well when he built his Red House at Upton. There must have been a nice view from its windows, though now it is surrounded by houses which will never have a history, and Upton is part of Bexley Heath.

Morris had just married the beautiful Jane Burden of Oxford, and so strongly did he feel about the awfulness of contemporary design that he decided to build a house and himself design furniture which should be worthy of it and of Jane. He had studied architecture for a year in the Oxford office of George Edmund Street, who later designed the dismal London Law Courts; and there had met Philip Webb and through him Norman Shaw, resuscitators of the corpse of good taste. The Red House was designed by Webb in a manner so advanced that it has ever since been a key building in the history of English architecture. It is, of course, surprisingly good for 1859, but I fear it is much flattered by photographs, which seem to suggest that all Victorianism had been eliminated from Webb's mind. In fact, it does look Victorian, but purged, purified, and forgiven.

The stretch between Dartford and Gravesend can hardly, I suppose, be called suburban; certainly not urban or rural; so perhaps maritime (but that is literally wrong, although the river is for sea-going ships) and industrial must do. Norman Shaw built one of his rather rare churches at Swanscombe, for the workers of the cement industry; Northfleet, too, is dusty with cement, and busy with paper-making; but Southfleet has still some villaginess a mile south of Watling Street.

I think Gravesend is generally maligned, and wonder if this is because its name is so dispiriting. For not only is it full of history: weighty in Domesday, fortified by Henry VIII, and celebrated in the annals of the naval shipyards; but it still has the qualities of ports, some romantic narrow streets leading up from the river, and all the special charm of shipping. This sort of purposeful riverside is, I think, the best of all for sitting in pubs and drinking beer on a fine morning. Here you can watch the Tilbury Ferry and appraise the liners and cargo boats and small craft from inns which have a proper naval tradition. There are, too, many good old houses throughout the town and a decided whiff of the Georgian nautical air.

St. George's church, which is suffering from war-damage, contains the grave of Pocahontas, the Red Indian princess. Her charming story reads more like a film scenario than history: the daughter of Powhattan in Raleigh's Virginia, she saved the pioneer John Smith from the clutches of her father's minions and helped the colonists with

Gravesend

advice, warnings, and food supplies. After Smith's return home she was taken as a hostage by the villainous English and told that her lover was dead. Accordingly, as a consolation or on the rebound, she married John Rolfe and went back to England with him, to be received at Court and taken up by society. It is said that she met John Smith in London and that the shock killed her. Whether that is true or not, she faded away romantically, and died at Gravesend in 1617 of the inevitable consumption. In America it is a happy boast to be descended, as was President Wilson's wife, from Pocahontas.

I was puzzled to find a seventeenth-century heroine buried in an eighteenth-century church, but apparently St. George's was burned down in 1731 and rebuilt in a rather grim and uncompromising Georgian style.

Gravesend has also an association with General Gordon, whom Lytton Strachey drew with Bible in one hand and brandy-bottle in the other—quite misleadingly, as it seems. He lived here while organising the Thames forts, and for six years devoted himself to the poor boys of the town, running a Sunday school and finding work, food, and clothes for them—all out of his personal pay.

From Gravesend to Rochester by main road is a cheerless journey except for a few stretches with views over the marshes of the Hoo peninsula and westward to the Downs. But it is worth having a look at Gadshill, where, as almost everywhere in this part of Kent, the Dickens tradition is dominant in the names of pub and tea-shop. Gadshill Place is a Georgian house, now used as a girls' school, on the main road near the scene of Falstaff's highwayman act with young Henry V. Dickens had coveted it ever since as a boy he had lived in Chatham; in 1856 he bought it; and died there in 1870. It is pleasant to know that the great Victorian, almost the same age as Gilbert Scott, must have retained from his youth the taste of the age in which he was born.

If you turn down the lane by Dickens's house you will come to a minute hamlet called Frindsbury Extra, almost in the V made by the Gravesend road and Watling Street joining at Strood. The "Three Crutches" is an admirable village inn among a smattering of cottages, but above it a few hundred yards away the London traffic roars to Canterbury and the sea.

The best village anywhere near is Cobham, a mile or two to the south-west; well deserving of its small fame. The Dickens content may be a little overdone, but I do not find the place much dolled up or artified. The "Leather Bottle", which comes into *Pickwick Papers*, has an interesting collection of Dickensiana, well arranged and decorative; and is a half-timbered building of the popular chaotic romantic sort. People are not so fond of the "Darnley Arms", which hides what I believe is an even older interior behind a painted Georgian façade. It has some landscape paintings in the bar, some of which I thought good and one almost beautiful. There were many more in various parts of the pub, all painted by Alfred James, who was for long the licensee and died in 1938. He was hardly one of those who "have a talent for painting", or are "keen on art". He could, without any training or ambition, paint; never taking the smallest interest in exhibiting or selling his work. The pleasantly ornate frames of his pictures, intricate mouldings and all, were also made by a Cobham villager.

The New College, which is behind and against the church, was originally built, in 1362, as a perpetual chantry for five chaplains; probably by Henry Yevele, King's Master Mason for the nave of Canterbury Cathedral. The hall of this foundation survives unaltered, but the rest of the buildings are a conversion of 1598, when the college was made into an almshouse for twenty poor persons. It is a perfectly delightful little place, which suggests that a half-cloistered community surely provides the good life for old people; and that much more ought to be done to ensure it everywhere.

Parts of the mediaeval church, too, were the work of Yevele, including the tower and the north porch. A more famous architect, Sir Gilbert Scott, was employed on what he called restoration by the sixth Lord Darnley, but he did not succeed in ruining the church altogether. It is famous, not for the architecture of any period, but for the magnificent collection of brasses—the best in the world—representing Cobhams from 1320 to 1529. Mr. Ralph Arnold has written a charming and authoritative book on Cobham and the Hayes family, *A Yeoman of Kent*; telling their story so well that it is now impossible to mention the place without cribbing from him. He says that the brasses are known as "lattens", a word derived from their metal alloy, and that they are set in Purbeck stone. The thirteenth-century chancel floor, therefore, displays at its best the unsophisticated convention of mediaeval drawing.

"The Street", as the main body of the village is known, is almost wholly unspoiled—set back from it is Mr. Arnold's own Meadow House, admirably built, and perhaps designed, by the Georgian Bonham Hayes in 1771—and from the lane which links it to Watling Street you get a good distant prospect of Cobham Hall, vast and comfortable in red brick. It is mostly sixteenth-century, but the west front is classic and probably designed by John Webb in the Inigo Jones convention—joining two Elizabethan wings and their lead-domed turrets.

My friend the unspeakable James Wyatt—he whom Pugin called "The Destroyer" and a "monster of architectural depravity" for his cathedral restorations—was employed here; most interestingly in designing the classic mausoleum in the park, one of his earliest works, and also, in his later Gothic phase, the entrance hall and staircase. Humphrey and George Repton were here, too, for great landscape-gardening in the grounds—George was also responsible for the "amusing" Gothic "Thong Lodge" at one of the park entrances. The mausoleum was never the scene of any burial, but it is an interesting example of the Georgian "sepulchral church", where a rich man could show off his taste while proclaiming his faith and the renown of his family.

In the park, too, are what are reputedly the tallest ashes in England, and in the house, mythically, "The Ashes" themselves—presumably only when our cricketers have vanquished the Australians. It was in 1882 that the latter, beating an England side by seven runs at the Oval, called forth from *Punch* the saying that the body of English cricket had been cremated, and the ashes taken to Australia. In the following winter, however, the English side which toured the burial-ground won the rubber narrowly and retrieved the remains. Their captain, always known in cricket history as "The Honourable Ivo Bligh", afterwards became the eighth Lord Darnley.

"Owletts" is at the extreme other end of the village; a middling-sized house of the late seventeenth century when taste was securely established in the classic phase. It is delightful with warm red brick and generous sash-windows; vast chimney-stacks, magnolias, and peaceful old garden; taken over by the National Trust, but still the home of Lady Baker. Sir Herbert, the collaborator with Lutyens at New Delhi, where I think he did his finest work, told much of "Owletts" in his autobiography *Architecture and Personalities*. It was built by Bonham Hayes, grandfather of Mr. Arnold's Bonham and of Richard the farmer-diarist; and bought after Richard's death by a great-great-grandfather of Sir Herbert Baker in 1790. Inside there is a very fine staircase hall with an intricate and exuberant plaster ceiling; the dining-room has chairs whose backs are carved each with a different device—one with owls for the name of the house, another with the head of one of Sir Herbert's daughters; and in the drawing-room an electric clock tells the time at home and in the Dominions and Colonies, each represented by an appropriate symbol—the Lion for England, the Anchor for South Africa.

From Luddesdown one objective is Meopham on the Wrotham to Gravesend road; with a pleasant green, a fairly well-preserved windmill, a good stout church of flint and brick, and some old cottages and inns—all rather a straggle. The interestingly named Tradescant father and son lived here; gardeners to Charles I and founders of our first natural history collection. Both were Johns, botanists, and scientists who accumulated the collection of Elias Ashmole, and so were responsible for a word—Ashmolean—which has become special to Oxford.

To go to Ash, Ridley, and Stansted is to plunge deep into the Downs at their most secret; free of the unseemly development which has made so much of the Pilgrims' Road into a suburban avenue. Ash Church and manor-house stand together in fields among great elms. The tower is plastered brick against a stone nave, and the Jacobean house, gabled and friendly in beautiful red brick, has been rather badly served by the wrong windows of a later date. But it is a happy little group.

Ridley is much smaller than Ash village; nothing but a little white-turreted church, an eighteenth-century house, and a farm; and Stansted is hardly more populous. In the enclosed hollow beneath the lofted church, Stansted war-memorial seems rather too ambitious for such a minute hamlet—an inscribed stone podium bears a bronze male figure carrying a palm.

East again, among still more tenuous lanes, you find Harvel, with some half-timbered cottages, and Vigo, where a camp took up much of the terrain during the war. Now, a new school, not at all successfully, apes the Cape Dutch with curved gables and apple-green roof. Much more natural and harmonious is the prospect of Fairseat on the other side of the Gravesend road; nearly 700 feet above the sea at the top of Wrotham Hill. It has an appealing conglomeration by a tree-shaded bend—a square red house seen across a garden; an aristocratic parapeted Georgian house on the road; and even a suggestion or two of "Gothick".

Wrotham Hill takes you very steeply off the Downs across the great London to Folkestone road, and into Wrotham village. There is breathing-space here before you get on to another main road, that which runs from Maidstone to the edge of the county at Westerham and far beyond. Poor Wrotham is badly hemmed in by the traffic lanes, but it is a pleasant place by the Pilgrims' Road, with a finely textured ragstone church—another objective of brass-rubbers; a manor-house and old cottages and shops; and some remains of an archiepiscopal palace. It once had fame, too, as a stopping place on the mediaeval route to Canterbury.

But we are going the other way at present, and before long get a good glimpse of St. Clere, a great Georgian house in a fine park. It is extraordinarily imposing: a very simple design whose vast scale seems more appropriate to a public building than a house; crowned by the most sensational phalanx of joined chimney-stacks I have ever seen. Soon the Pilgrims' Road becomes a long line of pretentious little houses overlooking a wide view, and one cannot feel oneself to be in the country on this ridge. Below it, Kemsing village has a pleasant spacious cluster of old church and cottages which barely escape the Pilgrim suburbia; and the agreeable Kentish surname of Wellbeloved is to be found. Heaverham village, too, is still rural, and the Tudor houses of Yaldham and Stonepits are near by.

I suppose it must be the station and the view from the Pilgrims' Road which have spoiled Otford with a rash of bad building. It is not, like Riverhead, a sort of suburb of Sevenoaks; nor is it attached to the London tentacles; it just spreads and spreads between Polhill and the lower slopes of the North Downs.

The real Otford is as sweet a village as you would wish; with a central green and a square-towered church by more palace ruins. This was the most magnificent of all the Archbishop's many mansions, but now there are only bits of a tower and chapel to suggest the building imagination of Archbishop Warham. It was probably the most favoured of the sixteen archiepiscopal residences, so naturally Henry VIII coveted it and got it, although Cranmer seems to have tried to put him off. The King stayed there on his way to the Field of the Cloth of Gold. Other Otford associations are with the

Church and Palace Ruins, Otford

Kentish family of Polhill—connected with Thomas and Oliver Cromwell and with General Ireton—which christened the hill dominating the Darent valley to the west; and, more anciently, with Roman river settlements, and battles fought by Offa King of Mercia and our Danish Canute.

Facing Otford Green near the palace ruins a Georgian range gives pattern to the prospect, and farther into the village in the direction of Polhill you can see some beautiful houses—the half-timbered one is as good as any in Kent; there is nothing "crazy" about its closely spaced upright timbers, silver-greyed and orderly; somewhat suggesting the East Anglian scene.

The Darent valley growing closely confined, Shoreham is sunk between two ranges of Downs in an unsullied landscape. There are fine trees along the roadside, and the little station is not such as to encourage unseemly domesticity. Above the village, a cross is cut in the chalk, and the church reflects the Downland geology in its flint mingled with brickwork. It is approached by a path between yews, and entered through an arch made out of a single great oak. Inside, Prestwick the geologist is commemorated in glass by Burne-Jones; there are representations of the Borretts, allied by marriage to the Polhills; and on the war-memorial are the names of the Puxty family, wiped out by Nazi air attack, among those of the men killed away from home. Wesley preached often here, at first against much noisy resentment but later with a regularity which must have implied acceptance. Blake came much to Shoreham, too, as the guest of Samuel Palmer, the painter, whose house is by the river. It is, I think, the nicest of the Darent villages: tortuous without being cramped, blessed with a bridge over the stream, and well off for pleasant houses and cottages and the sort of pubs where one may sit outside in the sun and contemplate the village scene.

Lullingstone, a little way north and still pinched in by the Downs, is a show place for silkworms, besides exhibits of more general interest. There is a Roman villa site which is still being excavated at the time of writing; showing a fine tesselated pavement designed round Europa, Bellerophon, and Spring. The horde includes a number of busts and the skeleton of a cat.

The estate has been in the hands of the Hart family for four centuries, but only the half-ruinous brick gatehouse justifies the name of castle. The house is late seventeenth- or early eighteenth-century; a rather unorthodox symmetrical composition in very beautiful red brick. There is a great grass space with cedars, and round it are grouped the house, the gateway, and the little church. A bit of a puzzle, the latter. At first sight it appears to be mediaeval, with a most inappropriate heavy classic porch foisted on it. Inside, the plot thickens, for the ceiling and much of the decoration is of early Georgian character. Has one been deceived—is this one of those rare and charming "Gothic Survival" chapels like Peterhouse's at Cambridge? No. The first impression was right. It was Sir Percival Hart who classicised the old church in the eighteenth century, and one can say that he did it successfully although the porch, surely, is regrettable. The outside of the church is almost white, washed over in some manner difficult to diagnose, like Fawkham church not far away. But its contrast with the house is readily acceptable.

I shall not say much about the silkworms—a subject for experts which is well set forth by the present owner, Lady Hart-Dyke, in her book *So Spins the Silkworm*; only that the little industry is well explained to visitors; that the yellow of the raw silk is incredibly lovely; and that the worms themselves have for me a rather pathetic sort of charm. Most appealing is their custom of sitting up to go to sleep, with only their nether portions in contact with their mulberry leaves. It is strangely touching, too, to listen to them eating, eating, eating. For it is about all they do. It is a sorry fate. For, after an extremely rapid growth, they weave their silken cocoons which most of them never leave alive. Those which do are put, as it were, to stud; and they are not much more to be envied. The moths, so hopelessly over-domesticated and specialised in their function, are blind and cannot fly. They can only flop and, of course, procreate. And that is their end.

The road follows the Darent to Eynsford, and the Downs recede somewhat. There are ruins of a Norman castle perhaps longer deserted than any, since it is said to have been uninhabited since the time of Becket; and a Roman villa site which gave up tiles bearing the footmarks of both man and dog imprinted in the damp clay. Eynsford has a famous little old bridge over the river and some half-timbered houses which are favourites of the photographer; and although the main street is unhappily developed almost into Farningham, and the high ground to the west has sprouted some poor building, the body of the village has kept its proper quality.

The London–Maidstone road inevitably destroys rurality and the continuity of the countryside through which it runs—that is the trouble, so far, with all our by-pass roads. A better controlled town-planning might have avoided this evil and may now prevent anything more evil still; but there is no doubt that some villages have benefited by the loss of traffic: Farningham, for instance, where Bligh of the *Bounty* lived at the manor house—peaceably after his involuntary voyage of 3600 miles in an open boat. (The manor was destroyed by enemy action, but there are still men called Christian on Pitcairn Island.)

The "Lion" is an especially attractive Georgian hotel by the Darent; red brick with a green copper window-hood; there is a fine mill-house, and the strange and lofty White House, black-painted on bays and odd Venetian windows.

You must, to follow the Darent, cross the great by-pass at Farningham, and perhaps fill up with petrol at the remarkable station which has a Cotswold stone roof, much lavish oak, and polished copper oil-cans. It will be obvious that you are getting back to Dartford, for although Horton Kirby at its southern end is snug by the little river, it tails off rather desolately into viaduct and factorial buildings to the north. East is the really nasty Longfield in the Gravesend purlieus, and you must go down to Fawkham to approach again the deep-laned Downland. But there are two more Darent villages to see before turning back into the Downs.

Sutton-at-Hone is, I am afraid, a rather depressing place; it escapes being a town and you can't say it is much industrialised; and yet village hardly seems the right word for it. It has, however, the National Trust property of St. John's Jerusalem, a pleasant place set within a moat in surroundings restful to the eye. Its history is of more than ordinary interest: first the manor of Robert de Basing; next, in 1199, given by him to be a Commandery of the Knights Hospitallers of the Order of St. John of Jerusalem; mostly pulled down in 1540, when the Order was dissolved; and rebuilt by Abraham Hill—a founder of the Royal Society, who spread the cider industry from Devon to Kent—in the seventeenth century.

Henry III stayed often at the Commandery, of which the thirteenth-century chapel remains; and, 500 years later, Edward Hasted the Kentish historian was the owner who hastened his bankruptcy by some Georgian improvements.

Darenth is a little way off the Dartford road to the east—the village has an h, the river not; I don't know why. It is much smaller and more villagy than Sutton; with a church containing Saxon work done with materials from a large Roman villa which was here.

According to my meandering plan, I have to go back to Eynsford and over the bridge, westward, up the hill into queer semi-downland country which seems, paradoxically, both remote and suburban. Narrow and forbidding lanes surprisingly generate shacks and bungalows, and at Crockenhill this strangely populated isolation is most emphatic. The way southward up Skeet Hill takes you into the most Londonward slab of the Downs, and from the top of Well Hill, where a mysterious house has a glass look-out on the roof, you can see great views eastward to the middle Downland range, and westward far into Surrey. This is the last hope of seclusion which, found in Chelsfield village itself, is soon lost on another arterial road cutting it off from its church and Court Lodge. Both are worth looking at—the church, in Downland flint and brick with a Jacobean monument to Peter Collet, is dedicated to St. Martin of Tours; the Lodge, a stout and comely red brick Georgian house in an old garden. But all around is suburbanisation, and the railway runs between two main roads heading for London; taking in Orpington and Petts Wood where the scene is no longer Kentish. To complete my London–Darent–Downland survey, I must cross both these main roads to Farnborough and make for Downe village.

The journey takes me back quite soon into a countryside which is little spoiled; up on the 500-foot contour; thickly wooded and deep laned; dry and chalky, without the lushness of the ragstone hills. Downe's fame is Darwin's, for he lived in the house, just ouside the village, where you can see his garden, laboratory, furniture, and scientific paraphernalia. A great deal of his research was done here—that work which, perhaps, involved a greater mental revolution than any other man's; destroying forever the neat and comfortable traditional beliefs in the creation of the world. Downe has changed remarkably little since the days of the great evolutionist.

Cudham is rather more built over, but not much. It has a more open site among the hills, and a quality of village decency. Here were born the Portingall quads in 1659, and now an early Victorian house of acceptable Italianate design is an offshoot of John Groom's Crippleage.

From these hills was witnessed a wonderful distant Hell scene as the blazing Crystal Palace, Paxton's inspired greenhouse which the German architect Erich Mendelsohn in the nineteen-twenties called the only modern building in England, staged a spectacular show for the residents on the Kentish Downs.

Knockholt Beeches are well over 700 feet up, and I am told that they can be seen from the Crystal Palace, from Leith Hill, and from Harrow. There are, at Knockholt, a green with a few pleasant houses; a "folly" of some kind, tall, square, and altogether without frivolity; and an old church restored. But I find Knockholt rather messy and incoherent, even though its station is miles away north of the Polhill tunnel.

Halstead is associated with "Boffins" and backroom research at the big house of Halstead Place; but only very discreetly in a pleasant village where all sorts of mysterious discoveries were made during the second world war, and, I have no doubt, continue to be made.

Along the Darent valley here the Downs are very steep, sloping southward at Brasted Hill and Hogtrough, which have wide views to the Ragstone Ridge, and, from some points, over the top of it. But I must keep that country for my journey home.

The Downs near Cudham

KENT
WITH HER CITIES AND EARLES
described and obserued.
Odo Bishop of Bayen
Will Iprese E of Flan
Hubert de Burgh
LONDON
Part of
essex
Southwark
THE
LATHE
OF
SVTTON
AT
HONE
LATHE
OF
AYLFORD
Tunbridge
Seuenok
Grauesend
Dartforde
Bromley
Wrotham
Malling
Maidston
Cranbrooke
CANTERBURY
SVSSEX
SVR
REY
PART
OF
THE SCALE of PASES

Map by John Speed, engraved in 1611; lent by P. J. Radford

3

Estuaries and Islands; Medway and North Downs

GRAVESEND and Rochester link the Thames and the Medway; and the water-girt piece of country to the eastward, an isolation of marshes, is the Hoo Peninsula. Its air of remoteness—although it is certainly not unblemished by building—derives from the fact that nobody goes there on the way to anywhere else. It is unpopular in the best sense of the word; without any seaside resort, or any natural beauty except for people with a taste for marshes and mud. The shipping which circumnavigates this coast-line, making for Gravesend, London, or Chatham, is not much concerned with pleasure, and the peninsula has no town of any sort.

The Hundred of Hoo—that is a far more poetic name for it—has no villages, even, which are comparable with the best of Weald or Downs. Here there is an air of melancholy, shabby and unwelcoming; of indifference to visitors and a strong isolationism.

There is Higham, with a partly Norman church, and the Abbey Farm where remnants of a convent of Stephen's reign moulder; Cooling with its stout castle gateway; High Halstow finely sited midway between Thames and Medway; Cliffe in the north and Hoo in the south.

Cooling claims both Shakespearian and Dickensian contents—the village has Pip in *Great Expectations*, and the castle Falstaff, who was evolved, libellously as it seems, out of Sir John Oldcastle, its owner. He was, indeed, a friend of Prince Hal, and by marrying into the Cobham family became its head; but his religious beliefs led him to Lollardry for which he suffered martyrdom in 1417. Cooling Castle was badly smashed up when Sir Thomas Wyatt captured it in his rising against Bloody Mary.

Now it is only a gatehouse and some tree-grown ruins; most imposing with fat circular machicolated towers; standing on the little village roadway as a reminder of history.

Yes, it is strange, this half-desolate country of marsh and estuary, so free from airs and graces that one would need to live long in it to love it. I can imagine an attachment to High Halstow, because its site would be a matter of some pride. Only 100 feet above the sea, it yet surveys enviably both the great estuaries, and buildings make use of the contour and fascinating orientation. The thirteenth-century church crowns the rise, and the "Red Dog", squatting near, has paint to match its title.

Cliffe, or more properly Cliffe-at-Hoo, is nearer the Thames mouth; quite a sizeable village for the Hundred; sited on a low chalk escarpment above the marshes. It has a surprisingly big church, mainly thirteenth-century with some Saxon odds and ends; a pleasant village street and some quiet little old cottages. But this, too, has strangeness—a lack of colour as if the Hoo landscape were done in monochrome—something almost foreign, and certainly not suggestible by the word Kentish.

Rochester Castle

For the rest, All Hallows is the most northerly; perhaps destined to become a seaside place as it spreads to the sea; Grain in the Isle of Grain, where streams and saltings wriggle between the sea and the Medway, is in the easternmost and least accessible part of Hoo; and there are Stoke, with its views across the estuary to Sheppey; and Hoo itself.

Or rather, Hoo St. Werburgh. For there is St. Mary's Hoo, and All Hallows is a Hoo, too. To say nothing of Cliffe-at-Hoo. It is rather confusing but true to say that Hoo is the chief village of the Hundred of Hoo. It is almost on the Medway where the great estuary narrows down by Hoo Salt Marsh and Gillingham Reach; so that the shingled church-spire is a landmark for seamen. The church itself has something of Saxon and Norman as well as of all the Gothic phases, and the corner where it stands is nicely secluded from a street more lively than is the rule in the Hundred.

Mr. Arnold Palmer, who wrote the excellent notes for *Recording Britain*, says that this terrain between the estuaries has a discouraged air. It is an apt word; expressing unwillingness to compete with more popular and populous countrysides. But, he tells us, there was a time when its fate might have been very different. The railway still runs from Gravesend through the stations of Cliffe and Sharnal Street and the halts of High Halstow, Beluncle, the Stokes, and Grain Crossing, to Port Victoria. This last was once a gateway to the Continent, called after and used by the Queen; intended to supplant

Queenborough and Tilbury and, when the Royal Corinthian Yacht Club was established there, Cowes. But these glories were shallow-rooted and soon withered, although Mr. Ralph Arnold in *The Hundred of Hoo*, tells us that the Kaiser touched down on a red carpet at Port Victoria on his way to the Coronation of George V.

Strood, Rochester, Chatham, Gillingham—only those who know them really well can tell where one ends and another begins. Their general prospect is decidedly chaotic; difficult to sift architecturally, to catch visually; and difficult, of course, to write about. What is good seems short of breathing space in a built-up area hostile to planning.

Yet there is a spirit or atmosphere worth catching; a muddled and almost indefinable charm—at least in Rochester and Chatham, the senior partners. Gillingham, too, touches the Royal Naval Dockyard; and Strood provides the famous view of Rochester Cathedral and Castle over the broad Medway; leading us to them over the hideous iron bridge to which few can be reconciled by mechanical sentimentalism.

Rochester Cathedral is, after Canterbury, our oldest foundation, and the Norman nave is magnificent; the west front, too, is out of the ordinary architectural run with its Norman mouldings and foreign-looking Romanesque turrets. But on the whole one has to admit that it leaves one decidedly cold. This is not because it is small by cathedral standards, but more by reason of the unpleasant grey and smarmy texture of most of the stonework. I don't know if this derives from a cement-laden atmosphere, but certainly one thinks rather more of Gilbert Scott, who, incidentally, let fly with his horrible tiles in the choir, than of Gundulph, Ernulf, and John of Canterbury.

And then, you can't say that Rochester has precincts like Canterbury, or a close like Salisbury or Winchester. In this confined city there is no room for such tranquillities; but there is some sort of haven round the cathedral—Thomas More's house, for instance, and the eighteenth-century Minor Canon Row, which is somewhat crooked in doorhead and sill but full of quiet good taste and the right sort of respectability.

Here, too, is the Prior's gatehouse, one of the city gates, and another beside which stands the teashop known as Edwin Drood's House. The parish church is up against the Cathedral, seemingly unnecessary but architecturally admirable. The school, in the midst of all this, is a mass of graceless Victorian buildings.

The prospect of the Cathedral from the other side of the river is greatly helped by the keep of the Norman castle; square and forthright with surmounting towers at the angles—a study in solid masonry rather than in architectural design. Here the barons were beseiged by King John, and it looks as if it could still stand up to a considerable assault. The public gardens which surround it, lofted above the esplanade, give you a fine view of the variegated Medway shipping.

There is the High Street, a busy and narrow jumble of every sort of building you can think of—two are especially good: the seventeenth-century Guildhall, with a gracious colonnaded front; and the Corn Exchange which was the gift in 1706 of our old friend Sir Cloudesley Shovel. Both might well be from Wren's drawing-board.

There are, too, Richard Watts's almshouses for poor travellers, and the extremely charming Eastgate House, which is now used as a museum. It must be late sixteenth- or early seventeenth-century.

St. Margaret's Street climbs the castle hill from the Cathedral; the quietest and most friendly part of the city, with a comfortable and tasteful Georgian air; looking down over the river to the tall industrial buildings, the cement works, and the Downs. St. Margaret's Church is an oddity, an exceptionally cold and crude late classic building jammed on to a medieval tower. It looks its best from the esplanade below, dominating the slope up to the ridge; neighbour to a romantic Regency house with a Gothick façade, which gives the prospect a picturesqueness acceptable to contemporary men of taste. But whoever put that stucco nave on to the ancient stone tower, and was not offended by its junction with the flat pitched roof, could not have been strong in that quality.

Rochester introduces the naval tradition, which is emphasised in Chatham; brings reflections on Admiral de Ruyter and the rude incursion of the Dutch against our unprotected fleet; and is full of almshouses and bequests concerned with naval charities. Of the almshouses, the most lavish and liveable are Thomas Hellyer Foord's, high up on the hill above the Borstal road. They were built in 1927 to the design of Guy Dawber; on the lines of a small red brick college with archway and central fountain. Everything is spacious and neat and carefully thought out, and I should think the people who live there are much envied. In the hall there is a picture of the men who brought it into being: Dawber the architect, Anning Bell and G. E. Moira, the artists, and Ernest Gillick, the sculptor—a fitting commemoration.

It is worth while having a look at the famous Borstal Institute, built on the top of a hill near the site of an old fort. There was a prison there before it, and some Rocastrians can still remember seeing chained prisoners; but the Institute was built in the first decade of this century to a surprisingly sensible and simple design in yellow brick. (Probably ornament was considered too frivolous and expensive for the job, and the buildings have benefited from that economy.)

Borstal village is joined to the city, but the southern end of it introduces the country at a point where the Medway has still a great span and the vision of shipping against the Downs. It was just about here that the Canterbury pilgrims made their crossing of the river.

Besides the chaotic building link-up, the Navy joins Rochester, Chatham, and Gillingham with a more acceptable bond. (Nor are the Royal Marines and some Army units to be forgotten.) This naval tang is, in fact, the predominant atmospheric element in the ancient Medway towns, and it is perfectly easy to imagine that they might, to anyone in Hong Kong or Singapore, take on all the nostalgic beauty of Canterbury.

At Fort Pitt, where there is a green open space up the hill beyond St. Catherine's austere little almshouses, one feels a change. This is Chatham. The Regency houses overlooking the Fort have a shabby grace and, somehow, an atmosphere and character different from anything we have seen in Rochester. You can go down one of several steep little streets into the High Street, where the Chatham identity is much more obscure. There is the Sun Hotel, more or less the counterpart of Dickens's "Bull" in Rochester, and the really delightful almshouses of Sir John Hawkins—the first Englishman to buy and sell slaves!—minute in scale and the sweetest of the lot. Many decent old houses jumble amidst the same narrow traffic jam, and the strange indefinable charm has increased its naval content. From the High Street, lanes and openings give glimpses of shipping on the river, and there is never any doubt about the purpose of the place.

Figure-heads in the Admirals' Walk in the Royal Naval Dockyard, Chatham

Its spirit is epitomised by the Royal Naval Dockyard, the core of the Medway estuary. Through the imposing archway you can see the dockyard church, typical of the sensible and comely, if rather unspiritual ecclesiastical architecture of the early nineteenth century; and also one of the great figure-heads from Admiral's Walk. They give a touch of colour and, almost, fantasy to the mass of sound utilitarian building which extends from the dockyard to some of the neighbouring barracks.

As early in the war as 1940, a German submarine came up the Medway to surrender. It was thought that this must be some subtle Nazi hoax, but no—after the guns had been trained upon the ship and an officer sent aboard to parley, it turned out true that this German crew had already lost zest for the war and welcomed imprisonment. Cowardice or good sense? Shame or triumph? The result of thought which could save the world, or of muddle-headedness? I don't know.

For the Isle of Sheppey, that other "discouraging" element of Kent, you must go down Watling Street through the Chatham–Gillingham suburbs to Rainham or Newington, both of which have some pleasant old houses in the uninteresting lay-out of a main road street. You get to the creeks and saltings quickest from Rainham; to the villages of Upchurch, with its extinguisher spire, and Lower Halstow, far isolated from its twin at Hoo. Upchurch has a Drake tradition, the sea-dog's father having been vicar here in the fifteen-sixties, so that Francis must have known the place. But I think Lower Halstow is better for views of the Medway creeks and islets. It has perhaps the most interesting marshland purlieus and the pleasanter village lay-out—Bobbing and Iwade are very ordinary villages, almost featureless between Medway and Swale.

The rather primitive-seeming Queen's Bridge spans the West Swale to take you into the island. Immediately there is the sense of desolation which is imaginative rather than actual. These great flat marshes are not really deserted or remote; there seems no possibility of getting lost, but only of being unwelcome. There will soon be signs, one feels, of a life which is not genuinely isolated. There are.

This is, of course, the most populous end of the island, dominated by Queenborough and Sheerness. The former, where the West Swale runs into the Medway mouth, is an old place with a few castle ruins of Edward III. He changed its name from strange Bynnee in honour of his Queen, Philippa of Hainault, making it into the smallest of royal boroughs; but its renown dwindled till the castle was pulled down in 1629, and by the eighteenth century it had become a humble settlement of the fishing and oyster industry.

Road and rail skirt the estuary to Sheerness, whose dockyard is of Charles II's time, when twelve guns commanded the Medway and that great Secretary to the Admiralty, Samuel Pepys, inspected the site with the King. Where Queenborough has hung on to an old Town Hall and some contemporary houses, Sheerness looks like any other uninviting seaside town. The shingled tarry beach and the layman's area known as Marine Town look north, past Grain to the Essex coast; but the Naval Dockyard faces across the river mouth, and shipping passing Garrison Point may be bound for Thames or Medway. Such places, I think, have their own valuable essence when they are concerned with defence or trade; it is when they set out to entertain—lacking the necessary nucleus of fashionable Regency building—that they fail to please. The estuary mud, the marshes, and the ships—these are of the proper quality in a melancholy landscape not without poignancy but unsympathetic to gregarious holiday-making.

Eastward, the coast-line rises to form 100 feet cliffs of clay which are always in process of being eaten away by the sea; and behind this escarpment lie the villages of Minster and Eastchurch, still at cliff-top level—south the land falls away again to the marshes of Elmley Island, Windmill Creek, and the Isle of Harty.

Minster's fame is the seventh-century convent founded by Sexburga, Saint and Queen of Kent. (Miss Dorothy Gardiner, in her *Companion into Kent*, says that for centuries Sheppey girls were christened Sexburga, and this is one of those occasions when one cannot but be glad that an old custom has died out.) The only coherent piece of old building is the gatehouse, but bits of the convent have been absorbed into the parish church. Eastchurch has a complete perpendicular church of 1431, built on land given by William Cheyney. His great house of Shurland Castle, near the village, had nine courtyards, chapel, and banqueting hall, but after Sir Henry Cheyney had let it decay, Queen Elizabeth took it over and turned it into a barracks. Little is left of it except two little towers, and one can only ponder the extraordinary casualness of the great landowners of the past.

There used to be a coast road from Warden to Leysdown but the sea took it, so now you must reach them separately from Eastchurch. Warden Point faces the Nore Lightship, and you can look across the Thames estuary or eastward along the coast to Thanet. Here, too, the land is being slowly raped, and the church of St. James, built early in the nineteenth century out of stones from London Bridge, fell with a slice of cliff into the sea. At Leysdown the Navy first flew, and the Wright brothers witnessed its tuition by

Charles Rolls and those Shorts who have made the flying-boat a native of Kent.

It is all marshes across the Isle of Harty, where Harty village is the most inaccessible in Sheppey. It has a Norman church, a farm or two, and some cottages; a view over the Swale ferry which takes you to Oare and Faversham. Harty church has the famous "Flanders Kist", a chest carved with a tilting match, probably of mediaeval German craftsmanship. All around on the marshes, cattle graze, supervised by the "lookers" who live scattered among them, and the marshland roads call on the traveller for much opening of gates.

Until some time in the fifteenth century, most of the shipping bound for London from the East went up the Swale; and Faversham was attached to Dover as a junior member of the Cinque Ports. There is still a certain amount of barge-borne trade in Faversham Creek—enough to give the old market town a maritime smack at its northern end. The narrow streets are full of old houses, and the market-place and broad town centre where the Guildhall stands is one of the pleasantest townscapes in Kent. Buildings on open colonnades have for me a particular charm, as if the lack of a ground floor enhances the keenness of imagination about what goes on upstairs. But they usually end by getting filled in, and then their character is quite changed. Here the substructure is sixteenth-century, and the solid top-hamper—a simple classic design in cream and brown—of the early nineteenth. The wide street running to the creek is full of good things, petering out rather sadly amidst obvious neglect as it approaches the waterway.

There is the Tudor Grammar School—here the ground floor of another stilted building has in fact been closed in—which is now used as a Masonic Hall; the excellent old harness-maker's shop hard by the Guildhall; some remains of a twelfth-century abbey; and an interesting parish church with an intricate spire. There is King Stephen, who founded the abbey and is supposed to be buried in the church. (After his war against Matilda he died at Dover, but somehow or other his body was thrown into a creek here for the sake of his coffin's lead.) There is, too, St. Crispin, a refugee from Diocletian's persecution, who settled in Faversham as a cobbler and so became the patron saint of his trade.

And there is Arden of Faversham, who lived at No. 80 Abbey Street; a rich man, clerk of the court and Controller of the Customs; murdered in 1550 by his wife and her lover. The story was dramatised in 1586, probably not by Marlowe—though some ascribe the play to him—who lived at Canterbury.

Faversham has been since Elizabethan times a manufactory of gunpowder—in the eighteenth century the mills blew up and wrecked half the town; and also, though less famously than Whitstable, an oyster-breeder; having its own dredging-ground in the creeks. And, of course, the great smuggling industry thrived here as in many other parts of Kent. But for me it is a comfortable, rather dusty and unsmart Kentish market town with some lovable buildings, an implicit historical sense, and some views over the marshes, the Swale, and the Isle of Sheppey.

From here I propose to go through the hideous suburbs and cross Watling Street into the country between it and the Downs; working my way round to main road and town again at Sittingbourne. Throwley and Sheldwich are joined by the history of the Sondes family, whose alabaster monuments—the kneeling figures of Sir Thomas and

1. *A typical stretch of the Pilgrims' Road where it becomes a track near Wrotham.* A. F. KERSTING

2. *The Darent at Eynsford.* STANILAND PUGH

3. *A fine Roman mosaic found at Lullingstone Castle in* 1949. THE TIMES

4. *Old houses at Gravesend suggest Clinker-built ships.* A. F. KERSTING

5. *Pattern and atmosphere : the view from Wrotham Hill.* J. CHETTLEBURGH

6. *Some of the brasses in Cobham church. They range in date from the fourteenth to the sixteenth century representing members of the Cobham family, and constitute the finest collection of brasses in the world.* COUNTRY LIFE

7. *Cobham College was originally founded as a perpetual chantry in 1362 ; dissolved by Henry VIII, it was refounded as an almshouse by Lord Cobham in 1598.* T. EDMONDSON

8. *Otford Church : solidity and repose.* LEONARD AND MARJORIE GAYTON

9. *Paper Mills. The industry has a long tradition in the Dartford area, where the first mill was set up by Sir John Spielman in 1607.* P. C. CLARK

10. *Otford : the ruins of the Archbishop's Palace have a beautiful texture of brick and stone.* J. CHETTLEBURGH

11. *Hall Place, Bexley, is a unique Tudor house on a much older site. It is strongly associated with ghosts, one of which is said to be the Black Prince.* FOX PHOTOS

12. *Charles Darwin's Study at Downe House, high up on the North Downs near the Surrey border.* CROWN COPYRIGHT

13. *Dickens achieved an ambition of childhood when he bought Gadshill Place, near Rochester. It is a Georgian house with some Victorian discrepancies. The great novelist died there in* 1870. J. CHETTLEBURGH

14. *Rochester Cathedral: the fine Norman nave.* CROWN COPYRIGHT

Opposite: 15. *Rochester Cathedral in the Medway city.* LEONARD AND MARJORIE GAYTON

16. *Chatham Dockyard : good taste and good sense in the architecture of utility.* WARBURG INSTITUTE

17. *Chatham : the house was once the Headquarters of the Captain of the Dockyard. The steps lead to Admiral's Walk, and must have borne Nelson on his way to it.* FOX PHOTOS

18. *Leeds Castle: a wonderfully impressive and coherent piece of mediaeval architecture, it lies moated below the Maidstone-Ashford road.* LEONARD AND MARJORIE GAYTON

19. *A pleasant composition at Bowley Mill, Boughton Malherbe. At the Manor House Sir Henry Wotton—poet, diplomatist, and architectural author—was born in 1568.* THE TIMES

20. *Faversham Guildhall: a good example of a "stilted" building with the ground floor still open.*
T. EDMONDSON

21. *Lees Court, Faversham: the magnificent seventeenth-century Italianate house ascribed to Inigo Jones. It was the home of the Lord Faversham who was unjustly blamed for the murder of his elder son.*
NATIONAL BUILDINGS RECORD

22. The Norman towers of Reculver church stand up dramatically between the sea and the flat cornfields of Thanet. The rest of the church was pulled down in the early nineteenth century, and the towers were preserved only because of their usefulness as a landmark for shipping. KENT MESSENGER

23. A perfect composition of stone, brick, and half-timber at Chilham. LEONARD AND MARJORIE GAYTON

24. The college of St. Martin and St. Gregory at Wye. Once both grammar school and charity school, it was converted in 1889 into the famous Agricultural College. COUNTRY LIFE

25. *Margate: Early Victorian boarding houses in Grosvenor Place still show some decency of pattern and composition.* FOX PHOTOS

26. *Broadstairs was much favoured by Dickens, who lived in the castellated building known as "Bleak House".* D. W. GARDNER

27. *Richborough was Caesar's fortified base of Rutupiae, a part of the fortifications set up by the Count of the Saxon Shore.* KENT MESSENGER

28. *The North Foreland is the easternmost point of Kent, and, apart from a piece of the Norfolk coast, of the British Isles also. The lighthouse is a design of stoutness and grace combined.* CROWN COPYRIGHT

29. *Ramsgate Harbour was thought in the eighteenth century to be the best in England: it was much concerned in trade with Russia and the East.* CROWN COPYRIGHT

30. *Form and pattern in the North gate at Sandwich, one of the Cinque Ports from which the sea has receded.*
T. EDMONDSON

31. *The eastern end of the sea-front at Deal—the pleasantest in Kent.* COUNTRY LIFE

32. *Deal, with Walmer and Sandown castles, was built by Henry VIII to defend the Kentish coast against invasion from abroad. It is planned on the design of the Tudor Rose.*
GRAPHIC PHOTO UNION

33. *Dover: the castle overlooking the early-nineteenth-century houses of Castle Street.* T. EDMONDSON

34. *Excellence of mass and texture at Dover Castle, one of the finest of the Norman period.* T. EDMONDSON

35. *A walk on the leas at Folkestone.* T. EDMONDSON

36. *Mersham-le-Hatch, built 1762–72, is the earliest complete country house by Robert Adam.* COUNTRY LIFE

37. *Barfreston has one of the finest small Norman churches in England.* WALTER SCOTT

Sir Michael and their wives—are in Throwley church. The Elizabethan Sir Thomas built the school, but Sir George, supporter of the Stuart dynasty, is the most interesting, because the most tragic, of the Sondes family buried at Throwley. He was made Lord Faversham for his services to the Royal cause, but his title died with him when his younger son Freeman, aged nineteen, murdered his brother George as he slept. Freeman was executed in 1655, and the crime was sensationally blamed on the father; certain morally indignant writers publishing a long list of his sins. He refuted their accusations and cleared his honour, however.

Sir George Sondes, or Lord Faversham, lived at Lees Court, which he replanned after a long spell in prison during the Civil War. The house is ascribed to Inigo Jones and could have been built by him in 1652, the last year of his life. It is not much like any other work of our first genuine architect, but no other name, except perhaps that of Sir Roger Pratt of Coleshill, comes to mind in face of those remarkable elevations. It is quite Italianate, with low-pitched roof and great overhanging cornice; but Mr. Sacheverell Sitwell detects the Louis Treize influence, and there does seem to be something French in the great range of tall sash-windows—thirteen on each of the two floors—separated by Ionic pilasters. There is great beauty in this richly simple design.

The approach to the fine park is by the hamlet of Sheldwich Lees, which lies outside the gates; protected on one side by woods and open on the other to the near Downland country. Its great green is fringed by a few old cottages, and I know of no sweeter introduction to a great house. Trees and fields are rich in this famous cherry-growing countryside, but character and geology change quickly as you rise to the 300-foot contour at Throwley and Badlesmere; and thence up into the true Downs above Charing.

Throwley has Belmont, the great house of the Harrises. It was improved in the spacious heyday of improvement by George, Lord Harris; son of a Brasted curate and victor of Seringapatam. Wounded in the head at the American battle of Bunker Hill, he is said to have arranged to watch the operation on his brain in a series of mirrors. The fourth Lord Harris was one of the grand old men of cricket; a great Kent player who was President of M.C.C. in 1895 and died in 1932. He it was who took an English team to Australia in 1878 to face the immortals Spofforth and Blackham, Bannerman and Murdoch. Mr. P. F. Warner tells how, at a humbler level, Lord Harris was a member of his team playing against Westminster School at Vincent Square. It was during the first war and the famous Kentish batsman was for a considerable time in partnership with a gallant commander who specialised in hitting fives. Lord Harris made twenty-one in excellent style and retired unbeaten. He was at that time aged sixty-six.

Eastling is another cherry-country village, a few miles to the east; enjoying a rather special local celebrity as the birthplace of Edward Hasted, the Georgian Kentish historian. He was most interested in the annals of families and properties throughout the county; carrying on a meticulous investigation for twenty years before publishing his four-volume *History of Kent*. He lived in Canterbury till his finances went so badly wrong that he had to be sold up; and died close on eighty as Master of the Hungerford hospital at Corsham.

The cherry country slopes from the Downs to the Medway and Swale; its soil as rich for barley as for fruit. But it has not the hop-gardens and oasthouses of the Weald on the other side of the Downs; nor, I think, the Weald's affectionate warmth of clay and oak. It seems to be a little blurred in configuration, soil, and building materials—its vision is not bright in my mind. In a rather secret territory of narrow criss-cross lanes, Newnham and Frinsted, Doddington and Milsted are pleasant enough; and Bredgar has a fine Norman doorway to its church. Near here, towards the Downs, I saw a gay and daring Georgian break with orthodoxy—a house whose parapet curved and curled over round-headed windows; and I liked Tunstall's cottages and a lovely old gabled house seen through a gate on the village street.

This is only a mile or two from Sittingbourne on Watling Street, where you get views over the Swale and Sheppey. One cannot say much for this two-mile-long main road town. It is not hideous, but it lacks the charm of Faversham; not obviously industrialised by its paper-making, yet deprived of the proper character of a market town by the volume of traffic which has no business with it. It is, in fact, a small port joined to the Swale by Milton Creek; and near it is the biggest cherry orchard in England—cherries were introduced here by one Harris who was fruiterer to Henry VII. But as you go through Sittingbourne, these things are too easily forgotten.

At this point I propose to take the Maidstone road across the Downs, bear left at Detling—famous for its R.A.F. station during the Battle of Britain rather than for its Norman church—and emerge near the London to Folkestone road at Bearsted. From this incredibly dull artery you can quickly reach some of Kent's best villages—I would not call Bearsted one of these in spite of its ample green, a famous cricket-ground where Alfred Mynn, the "Lion of Kent", once smote. But Hollingbourne and Harrietsham, Lenham and Charing are all high up on my long imaginary roll of merit. They lie close up to the southern slopes of the Downs, and from Hollingbourne the ascent is very sudden and steep, sunk in deep chalk and overshadowing trees; the lane runs over the top, through Bredgar and Tunstall, and down again to the Sittingbourne plain.

Hollingbourne is an admirable village of brick, tile, and half-timber on a devious plan. It has the manor house and Greenway Court, both connected with the great Kentish family of Culpepper which was so fatally mixed up with the affairs of Henry VIII. Both Anne Boleyn and Catherine Howard were related to it, and each was mistress of a Culpepper cousin—Catherine's Thomas came from Hollingbourne. The seventeenth-century Sir Thomas was in exile with the Stuarts and during twelve years of his absence his four daughters, according to tradition all beautiful, worked the celebrated Hollingbourne altar cloth in gold thread. Before the second world war, there was put up in the church a prayer for the safety of all those who should fly over it. "It appears to lie on the direct route to London from abroad." In 1940 the charity of parishioners must have been somewhat severely strained.

Nearer to Maidstone and south of the main road, Otham is full of good things, most famous of which is the National Trust property of Stoneacre, a good example of a fifteenth-century yeoman's house in half-timber. Loose, south-west, has its Wool House, also a Trust building of the same period; as well as an agreeable "Chequers" and Salt's Farm, orderly in yellow and brown among oasthouses and great cedars. But the chief charm of Loose is its precipitous clustering and the sense of secrecy among the lanes.

The Blacksmith's Forge at Hollingbourne

Leeds gives a glimpse of its magnificent moated castle from the main road, but one would need a personal visit, which I have not had, properly to describe it. Henry VIII was there with his first wife, already in contact with his second; Elizabeth was there as prisoner and as Queen; and in the seventeenth century it was the home of the Parliamentary General, Lord Fairfax, who was displaced in the supreme command by Cromwell, and later helped to restore the Stuart dynasty.

Here we rise to the Maidstone ridge, which is no relation to the Downs; taking in the Boughtons (Monchelsea and Malherbe) and Sutton Valence; and giving fine views over the Weald. It rises to 400 feet at the latter village, which is admirably sited on the slope, with a double village street—upper and lower layers of the ridge. There are some nice old cottages and the "Swan" is a charming pub, but I find here rather too much Victoriana for rural comfort, and the school seems too important for a village site with such wide Wealden views.

The bungaloid outcrops are virulent by Kingswood, where I was interested to see a signboard "The Battle of Britain"—interested because I once suggested, in a book on inn signs, that if they must be brought up to date, a Kentish pub might well make that particular change.

While on the subject, I must praise the Whitbread company for their interest in it. Lately, great numbers of their Kentish Houses have been given new signs which are mostly both ingenious and pictorial. More, they have issued a series of cards bearing the sign of each inn; so that if you stopped and drank enough beer in the right place at the right time you could complete a most instructive collection. The Whitbread colour-scheme, too—cream walls with brown paint and gold lettering—is a uniform befitting almost any village.

East Sutton Park has a magnificent site on the slopes of this ridge; Ulcombe Place, next door to its church, is almost as felicitously placed; and Boughton Malherbe, with fine views from the undulating ridge, has the manor house, reduced or promoted now to farm status, where in 1568 Sir Henry Wotton was born.

Poet, scholar, and diplomatist, he was educated at Winchester and Oxford; and after twenty years as ambassador at Venice, came home to take orders and the Provostship of Eton. He it was who said that a diplomatist was "an honest man sent to lie abroad for the good of his country", but I am more interested in another phrase of his coining.

Being a properly cultured man, Sir Henry considered that any gentleman should know something of architecture; his long term of office in Italy had made him familiar with the Renaissance attitude to art and the rule of Vitruvius; and in 1624 he published his book *The Elements of Architecture*.

He was very modest about it, saying that it was written while he was "troubled with a miserable stopping in my breast and defluxion from my head. It was printed sheete by sheete as fast as It was born, and It was born as soon as It was conceived." But his most famous contribution to architecture was his definition of its three principle attributes as "Firmness, Commoditie, and Delight". They have never been better described.

Hereabouts one has reluctantly to return to the main road in order to take in some more of the excellent villages which it by-passes or bisects. The more evil fate of bisection has befallen Harrietsham, but fortunately the best part of it is well concentrated south of the scene of the crime. It is really lovely, and its chief charm is the serene block of almshouses founded by Mark Quested of the Fishmongers' Company—the best I have seen in Kent. It is pedimented and parapeted; of a rich red brick set off beautifully, according to the excellent custom, by an inscription giving the date of founding as 1642 and rebuilding 1770—dates which are almost a guarantee of good taste. Opposite is a romantic half-timbered house of the best mediaeval breeding, and everything in this stretch of broad village street is pleasing to the eye.

Beyond the traffic artery, the other half of the village has been left with the church and the shops and the station; the lane thence takes you quickly on to the Pilgrims' Road and up into the Downs.

Lenham is by-passed, and south of it there is the fine country where the edge of the Maidstone ridge gives place to the Weald. To those who must reach the sea as fast as possible, it is only a name on an R.A.C. sign, but if you have time to stand and stare you will find a wonderful village square big enough for a large market town; with many half-timbered houses and the long comfortable lines of the "Dog and Bear", whose creamy façade with brown painted sash-windows seems to command the village. Lime trees guard the rows of little shops, and there is a sense of breathing freely, of spaciousness and light. Mary Honywood is said to be buried in the church—she who is mentioned in Foxe's *Book of Martyrs*, and had sixteen children, 114 grandchildren, 228

The Pilgrims' Road near Harrietsham

great-grandchildren, and nine great-great-grandchildren.

Charing is doubly by-passed, for it stands unluckily squeezed in the V made by the Margate and Folkestone roads. To live in this village must be like being a Red Indian in a reserve; for it is a place where the natives live in old houses and cottages, working in old shops and pubs, while the nameless horde sweeps by on both sides, ignoring and insulting them with the best will in the world. It can't be helped. It is ridiculous to bemoan the fact that there is no time to stop and look. One can't go everywhere. But in Charing you wish that the needs of fast transport could have been met a little farther off. Yet, for all I know, the inhabitants may rejoice in their accessibility; in the ease of getting on to a bus for London, Margate, or Folkestone.

The village street is full of good sense and good taste, and behind the church tower there are ruins of yet another archbishop's palace where Cranmer lived; inevitably taken over from that discreet prelate by Henry VIII, and another scene of his sojourn on the way to the Field of the Cloth of Gold.

I split the difference between the by-passes, bisecting the triangle by lane to Pett Place, a fine house with a seventeenth-century façade of Dutch gables and sash-windows, overlooking through elegant gate-piers a large green used for football. And thence to minute Westwell, sweet and snug in lanes overhung with trees; and on to see the odd gateway of Eastwell Park—all crusted in flint and yellow stone by a Gothick lodge. The house is nineteenth-century, in a fine park with a great forty-acre lake, beautifully sited. It goes back to the Elizabethan tradition of the Moyle family, and, long before, Richard Plantagenet, a natural son of Richard III, is said to have lived and worked as a bricklayer on the estate.

Boughton Aluph leads you by its broad green back into the Downs and on to the Charing–Canterbury road; and Boughton Lees, set back from Eastwell Park with old cottages on another green, is on the lane to the Stour and Wye.

The famous agricultural college of Wye dates from the fifteenth century, when its purpose was ecclesiastical, and you can see some remarkably interesting bits of building

The old "Flying Horse", Wye

of that time: silvery-grey stone lower storey walls, with cusped window-mullions, surmounted by rich red brick eighteenth-century upper storeys. The effect of this flukey union is extraordinarily attractive.

The College of St. Martin and St. Gregory was both grammar school and charity school until 1899, when the smooth Georgian and the crusty mediaeval buildings were adapted to their present function. A new gatehouse and quadrangle were built—certainly collegiate in form; but the best one can say for them is that they do not really spoil this excellent village. Plenty of nice old houses and pubs gather round the fat church tower and the collegiate centre.

The college founder was Cardinal Kempe, a native of Olantigh about a mile away. In his time the twelfth-century church was much bigger than it is now, for in 1686 the steeple fell down while a service was being held, destroying a large part of the building. The officiating parson was quick of perception and action: noticing a strange tremor of the bell-ropes, he managed to get the congregation out of the church just in time.

The barber's daughter, Mrs. Aphra Behn, was born at Wye in 1640 and lived to become our first professional woman writer. She was also an abolitionist and a spy; writing a novel against slavery and reporting from Antwerp the arrangements for the Dutch naval expedition up the Thames; but apparently the Admiralty didn't believe her, and she gave up spying for literature, producing many novels and plays of fair ability and typically contemporary low moral tone.

I think Wye is beautifully suitable for a residential college: the village setting should encourage an agricultural outlook in the way an urban university might not; there should not be more distraction than is encountered in country pubs, although perhaps some on the race-course; and it is the sort of place where a country life might best be lived. On the Downs above, students cut in the chalk the large crown which commemorates the coronation of Edward VII; and from the Downland road on the top you find one of the vastest views in all Kent. To the south-west there is no high ground between this vantage-point and the sea, but only the great stretches of the Weald and Romney Marsh.

But before we go where the view lures, there is Godmersham on the Stour between Wye and Chilham. It is a fine Georgian house and one of the Jane Austen places—not personal to her like Steventon, Chawton, and Winchester, but very much in that gentle, wise, humorous and pleasantly malicious picture which is made up of her work and her life. Godmersham Park was left to Edward, one of Jane's brothers, by his Knight cousins who adopted him, and whose name he took. Jane was often there, and her fondness for Kent finds a place in her immortal repertoire—she seems well in the running for the honour of being our most popular novelist of all time.

Above the park is Juliberry's Grave, where a Roman general called Julius Laberius is supposed to be buried in a Stone Age Long Barrow.

4

Seaside, Thanet, and North Downs

I WILL not pretend an unfelt affection for the Kent coast. It has suffered too much from unbridled builders to inspire devotion in anyone whose past happiness is not specially bound up with it; or who, never exiled abroad, has never therefore yearned for the White Cliffs.

For me its interest is, then, historical and architectural; not an affair of landscape or sentiment; so that I cannot but stress its immense importance in English history and some of the buildings which have played a part in it.

Approaching the sea from Faversham, one chooses perhaps the most unfortunate introduction. Hoo, Sheppey, and Swale we have credited with some melancholy charm of marshes and little ships—one can forgive them their muddled accretions for their purpose and their history. But Seasalter, once a real village, has grown into an unhonoured avenue of shacks and bungalows by the mile, leading to Whitstable and prejudicing the visitor against it before ever he arrives. The oyster town itself is sadly spoilt, although its eastern end has some agreeable conglomerations of boat-building, old weatherboarded cottages, and small workshops. Part of the beach, too, resists the epithet of seaside, and proclaims its part in an ancient and epicurean industry.

For Whitstable's oysters were known and savoured by the Romans, and I understand that its natives are now the best in the world. Instead of bungalows and caravans and hideous hotels, the oyster beds have given Whitstable some of the pleasant paraphernalia of the sea—the oyster fleet, the homes of the fishermen, and the ropes and the baskets and the tar.

The industry is run by the Whitstable Oyster Fishery Company, almost a family business founded on an eighteenth-century Act of Parliament; presided over by the Water Court of traditional dignitaries. I wish I had Mr. Richard Church's connoisseurship. He says that the flavour of an oyster has a metaphysical content. "It is not fishy, it is not substantial. It is a cleansing. It wipes away the taint of the world and the flesh from our palates. It prepares the way for the most superlative of vintages. It keeps us sober, yet it makes us susceptible." How excellently the poet unites the spirit with the flesh; joining by implication in Mr. Belloc's magnificent damnation of pleasureless Puritans.

Whitstable has, too, the small distinction of having received the old Invicta which, chugging out of Canterbury, where it is now in retirement, drew here the world's first passenger train through the world's first tunnel—an enterprise of the great Stephensons which never paid its way but wrote a paragraph in the history of the Industrial Revolution.

Herne Bay has an immensely long sea-front, part of which has some excellent Regency houses to give an idea of what the place was meant to be. That project never quite

Washing the oysters, Whitstable

came off, or it might have rivalled Brighton architecturally; it has not the fashionableness of Folkestone or the popularity of Margate, but I would choose it before either of them for a short stay.

Thanet was made an island by the channel from Reculver to Richborough, now represented only by the river-beds of Wantsum and Stour; but though the sea gave place to river it encroached upon the open coast-line, destroying the town of Reculver to wash against the walls of the church. Only the beautifully preserved twin Norman towers and a few much earlier fragments remain, overlying the Roman fort of Regulbium and the Saxon palace of Aethelbert. An eighteenth-century print shows the fine church with spires visible from far out to sea, but I think the towers' neat sturdiness is better uncapped. It is, however, regrettable that the church itself was pulled down in the early nineteenth century, when the great wall was built against the sea's onslaught. Had it not been for Admiralty solicitude for the landmark, the towers too would have been lost to us. One has only to glimpse them, magnificent, mysterious, and enticing, across the great flat lands of Thanet, to understand what a loss that would have been; and when you get close up to them you find that their texture is worthy of their silhouette. The coastguard station and cottages, hard against the ruins, have restraint of form, and the pub called after Aethelbert is seemly.

The great new road to the sea is what makes the flat Thanet cornfields seem transitory —a countryside traversed by those who would be somewhere else; expressive of the damnable quality of the by-pass for which I can see no mitigation. But in a lane from

Reculver you can see a really remarkable Elizabethan gateway in brick, which introduces a very ordinary house only about 100 years old. Something grandiose must have been here and is now vanished; the introduction, as at Cooling Castle, survives only to stimulate the imagination of lost glories.

This remoteness of landscape and architectural guess-work is soon destroyed by the great road which wants to take you as quickly as possible to Margate or Ramsgate, and ignores and insults on the way St. Nicholas-at-Wade, a real village with a Norman church among farm buildings and cottages. But, of course, if you are going by car to the coast, you want to get there fast; through Birchington village, where Rossetti is buried; attached by many hotels and boarding-houses to Minnis Bay; and Westgate-on-Sea, which, no doubt through an old personal prejudice and experience, I think of as consisting almost entirely of preparatory schools. This coast is, in any case, an excellent one for children, since the beach is sandy and there are many safely explorable caves in the cliffs.

Seaside towns are generally judged by the density and quality of their visitors rather than by their pictorial or architectural merits. They get good or bad names, therefore, in the social lists, and everything which is of interest about them, as towns, tends to be ignored. In the manner of fashion, it becomes the mark of superiority to go to Frinton, and of shame (except among perverse highbrows) to patronise Blackpool. Torquay is for people who have plenty of money but do not make it too obvious; Brighton is a mixture of those who have and do, and of residents lingering on from the old distinguished days; Eastbourne is much above Hastings in the social hierarchy; while in our Kent, Folkestone might be on nodding terms with Deal and can hardly withhold respect from historic Dover, but would not care to be seen speaking to Margate.

I always try not to start new cults for no one to follow; deploring the wooing of holiday-camps and detective stories by intellectuals; opposing the current campaign of general rebunking. I try, too, not to pile on blame where blame is expected, and strive valiantly to be sensible.

So I will not pretend that I like vast crowds—as crowds, nor enjoy a closely confined session on the sands; nor feel at home in fun-fairs or on merry-go-rounds. But I will say that Margate is very much maligned, and that if you look at the place itself instead of deploring amusements which you do not share, you will find a pleasant range of eighteenth- and nineteenth-century buildings along the sea-front as it curves round the harbour. The Dreamland amusement-centre, it is true, pierces the horizontal with its flat tower, but it was designed by an architect who knew what he was doing, and it is, in itself, a seemly advertisement.

The town is built on hills of chalk, and the eastward ascent, overlooking the sea, rewards you with the sight of Fort Crescent and Fort Paragon—excellent ranges of simple, unpretentious houses of the late Golden Age. (Beyond, as in other towns, social superiority involves architectural vulgarity, and the great hotels of Cliftonville are best forgotten.) But nobody should think there is nothing worth seeing in Margate.

The North Foreland is the most easterly point in England except for a part of the Norfolk coast, and in the knob of Kent between Margate and Pegwell Bay the traveller is bewildered by the sunset and the points of the compass. From many points, indeed, it is easy to imagine that Thanet is still an island—the sight of the encircling sea suggests, to those whom it has so often saved, not confinement, but freedom.

Yet in July 1949 the pleasant little town of Broadstairs, compact with old houses and narrow streets above the cliff-bound bay, feted a commemorative invasion. The Danish

Broadstairs Harbour

model Viking ship *Hugin* had been rowed over the North Sea 1500 years after the landing of Hengist and Horsa. I am not as a rule very fond of pageantry, but this was an idea which caught the historical imagination. It didn't matter whether the modern Danes were really of the stock of Hengist, or whether 449 was the true date of his landing; the Englishman's natural admiration of Scandinavian civilisation—surely a model for the world—predisposed the crowds to a welcoming mood. An act representing the Spanish Armada sailing up the Channel would not have induced the sentiment I felt at Broadstairs; nor even the appearance of a fake Caesar at Deal. For, as the crew of the *Hugin*, with her red and white striped sail, put on a spurt to beach her in the bay, I ran and cheered. And when the bearded braves jumped ashore and gave their cry of "Hil! Hil! Hil!" I was moved. Prince Georg personally underlined, by his unpretentious bearing, all the strongest arguments for monarchy; speaking with charm, modesty, and humour, and later unveiling a stone to mark this visit and possibly the spot near Ebbsfleet where the original landing took place. Dickens spent much happy time at Broadstairs—it has its "Bleak House"—and I think this jovial pageantry might have appealed to his vehement theatricalism.

Pegwell Bay almost certainly received Hengist and Horsa, and with its low cliffs to the west and easy gradient to the Minster Marshes, it would have afforded them some protection against the weather—coming by invitation, they needed none against the natives—and fair access to their new territory in Thanet. Even now Pegwell Bay is one of the nicest parts of the Kent Coast; pleasant in configuration and not much spoilt by building. You can see a great stretch of sea due east across the Channel or south along the Sandwich Flats.

Having overshot Ramsgate, I might as well at this point go inland to Minster-in-Thanet, where the Abbey has Saxon remains, and a fine Norman church links up with a little Saxon tower. Minster Court, too, has Norman work—a rarity in private houses.

Monkton, too near the monotonous main road, has a thirteenth-century church beautiful outside but rather dull when you go in; and the churchyard has many of those odd tombs so often found in Kent: tapering cylinders of stone vaguely suggesting the human shape. I don't know the origin of this rather crude conventionalism.

Monkton and St. Nicholas church towers rise nobly above flat fields rushed across by the sea-bound road, but it is possible to work your way back to Ramsgate by Acol hamlet and a network of lanes.

In the eighteenth century the newly completed harbour of Ramsgate was thought to be the best in England, busy in trade with Russia and the East. There are still some buildings of that time clinging to the town, but on the whole the front has been more vulgarised than Margate's, although it stands higher in the social scale. There are, however, some agreeable Regency town-planning schemes above the harbour, and the coast configuration and changes of contour up the hill give interest to the prospect.

Ramsgate has a sculpture of Augustus Welby Northmore Pugin, but his real monument is St. Augustine's Abbey, of the Benedictine Order, on the West Cliff. Next door is his own house, flint-built, gabled and spiked against the grimness of the Abbey. The tower of the church has the square simplicity of a genuine mediaeval building and the interior detail is better than what came out of Pugin's teachings.

He died here and is buried in the Abbey, his own church designed and paid for by him without the interference of cheese-paring clients; so that it and the house are probably the only buildings which were realised as he wanted them. (He could not altogether have approved of his own best work—the detail of the Houses of Parliament—since that was a Gothic skin over a classic bone-structure, and he was not a man who compromised easily.)

Poor Pugin! He thought himself a failure in spite of a vast practice and the authorship of several influential books. Artistically, of course, he was a failure; and prophetically a disaster; for his teaching, which equated art with morals and mixed up architecture with his personal conversion to the Church of Rome, resulted in the most hideous buildings of all time. He, and not Ruskin, was the true father of the Victorian Gothic Revival, and although he met with much opposition, including Ruskin's own, his moralising precepts were all too successful. He who raved against Wyatt "The Destroyer" himself destroyed a great architectural tradition where Wyatt disturbed some bones, spoilt some bits of four cathedrals, and encouraged the "amusing" Georgian Gothick trend. Pugin died mad, at the age of forty, from overwork and anxiety, leaving his successors to do a great deal worse than he had ever done.

The Cinque Ports date from the time of the Norman Conquest, when their purpose was to provide most of the ships necessary for the defence of the country against continental attack. Sandwich is the most northerly of the five and, like New Romney, farthest to the south, it has lost the sea; gaining, in the compensation of anti-climax, two famous golf-courses in the marshes. It is not a place one would easily associate with the Royal and Ancient, or any other game; but a specially attractive market town with snug and secret corners full of old houses; the ancient churches of St. Peter and St. Clement; the North Gate and the Fisher Gate, and St. Bartholomew's Hospital; and something of

The coast at Ramsgate

the charm of Rye (a place attached to and accorded the privileges of the Cinque Ports). Sandwich was the scene of Canute's landing in 1016 and, much later, shared with Rye and many other English towns the honour of receiving refugees from continental religious persecution. Like them, it received in return for hospitality a great wealth of industry and architectural graces from the admirable Flemish cloth-workers who came to our country. All this seems to be summed up by Manwood Court, grey and vague and romantically gabled on the road leading to Wingham and Canterbury.

Richborough, Caesar's fortified base of Rutupiae, is by the Stour, a little way north of Sandwich; a stronghold whose concrete foundations go thirty feet deep to support buildings of which nobody knows what was the purpose. Some ruins of the castle still stand and there is the site of an amphitheatre; but in spite of a great slab of walling which has been pictorially likened to a stranded whale, this is an archaeologist's place rather than an artist's or architect's. And of course a historian's. Built at the beginning of Watling Street, it was a vital link in the anti-Saxon fortifications set up by the Count of the Saxon Shore; and so important was it that the western coast of England was known as the Rutupine shore and garrisoned by the whole of the second legion of Augusta. It was also a centre of the Roman oyster industry. But in the year 410 the Emperor Honorius withdrew the legions to fight the Goths at home; and Richborough and Britain were left to the horrors of Saxon pillage and the long Dark Ages.

Between Sandwich and Canterbury, Ash is a pleasant old conglomeration of village building, and Wingham one of the best of all the eastern villages: big enough to buy stores in and amenable to slow evening walks in the broad street—a place to live in. The best home would be the soft red brick Georgian house on the western edge, whence you could see open countryside and yet be in and of the village. It has grace and urbanity and yet is friendly and rural.

Littlebourne is almost as charming, and it has for me the special interest of Lee Priory whose charm, alas, has vanished. It is a key-building in the history of architectural taste: originally a simple seventeenth-century house, it was amusingly Gothicised about 1780 by Pugin's bugbear James Wyatt. Contemporary prints show that he did it amusingly enough; and when I went there I expected to be amused. But just as, when Pugin went to Lichfield Cathedral he found that Wyatt had been there before him, so I, arriving at Lee Priory, discovered that Gilbert Scott had interposed himself between Wyatt and me. The result is a seventeenth-century house Gothicised by Wyatt and re-Gothicised by Scott; and it is anything but amusing. Wyatt's interior decoration, however, was for some reason left alone.

There was something in a new way shocking about the "Baedeker" raids of 1942. Up till then it had been possible to argue that only military and industrial installations had been attacked, and indeed the ruinous parts of London suggest that this was largely true. But Bath, York, and Canterbury! Their hurts must have been intended to wound in a manner more refined. Canterbury had, of course, for long been under the aerial battle-field of Britain, subject, like all of Kent, to the inaccurate aim or the jettisoned weapon. Now it became a selected target. And yet, terrible as the raids were, the onslaught must have been half-hearted; as if a superstitious awe of such a place were mingled with the Nazi sadistic sentimentalism; else, why not the dreaded obliteration of Oxford and Cambridge, city and town most precious of all?

Canterbury cannot compare architecturally with those two, nor even with one or two other cathedral cities; but it perhaps epitomises more exactly the history of England and English Christianity. We have appreciated that Kent was already the most civilised part of England when the Romans came; they fortified their city of Durovernum with a wall, and had a church, possibly on the Cathedral site, which Aethelbert gave to Augustine in 597; St. Martin's, too, may be the oldest church in England, since there is Roman work mixed up with Saxon; and the German bombs have revealed, amongst other archaeological finds, a Roman tesselated pavement near the cathedral.

Canterbury's main street runs more or less straight through the simple yet disorderly mediaeval plan, changing its name as it goes: St. Peter's Street, King's Bridge, High Street, St. George's Street; at right angles to the Stour. The Georgians, callous of antiquity, destroyed five of the city gates, leaving only the West, but much of the containing walls survive, and parts of the castle where once were incarcerated the Jews persecuted and expelled by Edward I. Bloody Mary preferred Protestants as victims of organised cruelty, and they too were here. The strange mound with the monument on top, called the "Dane John", is supposed to be the burial place of some substantial Romano-Briton; and the Chapel of St. Pancras, in the grounds of St. Augustine's Abbey, may have been a temple turned into a church by Aethelbert. (Most of the abbey itself is a missionary college built in the sham-mediaeval style of 1848—by Butterfield in one of his less violent moods.)

I think that distant views of countryside from which a great building rises against the skyline are the most beautiful of all—you can see Oxford so from the hills of Elsfield and Stow Wood; and from Tyler's Hill, although it is only about three miles from the city, there is a view of Canterbury Cathedral. There Mr. Aubrey Waterfield sat drawing it for *Recording Britain* on 31 October 1942, when waves of German bombers streamed over him on their damnable mission.

But the direct opposite—the framed accidental near glimpse—is best got from High Street as you look down Mercery Lane. The great cathedral, lacy-grey and triple-towered, rides magnificently above the city's narrow and devious streets; a little too closely confined, although new visions have resulted from the tragedy of 1942, and you are not often without the sense of its domination. Mercery Lane is, too, the proper line of approach to the precincts through the Christ Church Gate, which stands at the end of Burgate Street. The gateway has lately been restored and given back some of its mediaeval brilliance (if 1507 is mediaeval) by a skilful use of heraldic colour. Its figure of Christ was lost to the Puritan fanatics who also destroyed many of the niched sculptures on the Cathedral itself, but its decay has been excellently arrested, and it has all the comfortable majesty of some great college gateway.

The Precincts have a few enviable houses and even a discreet shop or two; and some out-buildings which have been turned into flats for ordinary laymen and laywomen who have been "precinctified". (I am indebted to Miss Dorothy Gardiner's *Companion into Kent* for the word.) But I have to admit that this gracious place, with the Archbishop's Palace and the King's School sheltering under the great cathedral, has not the wide serene loveliness of Salisbury Close, nor any comparable domestic architecture. The central tower, "Bell Harry", is lord of it all; not easily rivalled by any other of the late fifteenth-century; so that from the precincts the vision of Canterbury soars, and at ground level is not of much account. It descends somewhat to take in the twin western towers, one of which was well rebuilt in 1831; and, with perhaps still more affection, the neat and decorative Norman essay of Anselm's Tower.

The present cathedral was begun by Lanfranc in 1067 after the Romano-British and Saxon versions had been destroyed by Danes and by fire. The complete Norman building, too, was soon attacked, the choir of that being burnt down in 1174, only a few years after the murder of Becket. There came upon the scene the two master builders, William of Sens and William the Englishman, who rebuilt the choir in Early English; and, after two more centuries, the Norman nave was demolished and more fashionably recreated in the Decorated Gothic phase.

Mr. Church has much to say about how the Canterbury Pilgrimages, after their peak in Chaucer's time, gradually degenerated into a disgusting superstitious commercialism until Henry VIII put an end to the shrine of Becket. Summoners and pardoners and quacks abounded, and the shortages of food and accommodation induced by the vast concourses of pilgrims gave rise to a mediaeval Black Market on a flourishing scale. That spirit is gone, and some think that the good which was intermingled with it has gone too. Faith, creed, and dogma have lost much of their power, but there are still the touch and flash of the awareness of good. That awareness, I think, is the true meaning of all great art, and it is not an affair of definable beliefs. It may, indeed, be granted to the consciously faithless as well as to the typically twentieth-century doubter.

St. Martin's Church, Canterbury

It will descend on many as they enter the Cathedral and stand looking up the vista of the great nave, bringing with it the conviction that goodness is absolute and not merely relative. And not, of course, to be found unmixed. It is unlikely to be true, what Pugin thought, that mediaeval church-builders were habitually good men inspired in their work by the love of God; and we know that rakes and liars may be the creators of beauty. But something good in them there must be, however fleeting and inconsistent.

In a place like Canterbury Cathedral, you need something difficult to achieve—solitude. Guides and guide-books destroy awareness of this idea of good—more precious than facts. Those can be learned afterwards; the second or third visit is the time for discrimination at Becket's Crown, the Martyrdom, the Norman chapel in the crypt, the tombs of Henry IV and Joan of Navarre, of the Black Prince and of Archbishop Henry Chichele, founder of the unique college of All Souls at Oxford. There is the little chapel of Edward the Confessor, and the newly-painted and gilded St. Michael's Chapel, special to the Buffs. And innumerable monuments and architectural details of every sort.

All this wants a book of its own, neither too stodgy with facts nor too metaphysical with speculation.

In the city, I like especially "Queen Elizabeth's Guest Chamber", now a teashop with ornate plasterwork and intricate fenestration; and "the Weavers"—houses literally rising out of the river by King's Bridge; reminding us of that great Kentish cloth-working trade which absorbed so many Flemish and French refugees from religious persecution.

The West Gate makes a wonderful entry into the city, and I would go through it—

since cricket has for me a nobility not incompatible with its spirit—during the Canterbury week, when flowers and flags hang from crooked façades.

Kent cricket is part of the county history, after all. Frank Woolley and Colin Blythe were artists in their kind, and now we have the agile genius of Godfrey Evans behind the stumps. There is goodness of a sort in these things, and I like to remember that when the Canterbury Festival began we had the greatest county side till then known, headed by the ponderous "Lion of Kent".

With five such mighty cricketers,
'twas but natural to win,
as Felix, Wenman, Hillyer, Fuller
Pilch and Alfred Mynn.

With the old rhyme, I leave Canterbury. It will not blame me for frivolity if I think there of Alfred Mynn as well as Augustine and Becket.

The Canterbury landscape does not compare for me with the rich Weald or the ragstone slopes, but it provides a background of cherry orchards and low hills for many distinguished villages. Chartham has a green and Chilham a square, and round these voids the old houses and cottages squat in solid comfort. There are hints of a Roman downland fort at Chilham, and the castle is successor to one of Caesar's. The Norman Keep survives, but like Lullingstone and Mereworth, Chilham is not really a castle at all, being largely the work of our first authenticated architect, the classic innovator Inigo Jones. They say that from it you can get that coveted distant view of Canterbury Cathedral.

One way back to the coast is through Chartham Downs, by way of Lower Hardres, to Patrixbourne; or you can deviate farther south to Petham, a pleasant village in deep Downland whose church tower shows tender pink across the fields. But Patrixbourne is more of a show village. Its Norman church is sited by the road in a garden churchyard, and the entrance doorway is semi-circled by some very elaborate and, for the Normans, delicate decorative mouldings. It is beaten only by Barfreston, nearer the sea at Dover, for the Norman prize. Patrixbourne has Bifrons, the great house in the park, and some very charming cottages, of which a few are in the Romantic Regency gabled style.

A few miles farther down the Dover road, Bishopsbourne has the homes of two famous writers, one on each side of the church. Richard Hooker, the Elizabethan theologian and author of the *Laws of Ecclesiastical Polity*, was five years rector here; and, in our own times, Teodor Jozef Konrad Korzeniowski, the Polish merchant seaman, settled down in Bishopsbourne and, using his two middle names, made himself into a master of the English novel.

I went by way of Bridge, Adisham, and Chillenden through an open half-Downland country of tortuous lanes where you sense the nearness of the sea. There is Goodnestone, well known to Jane Austen as the home of her brother Edward's wife. The great house obligingly allows the road-traveller a fine distant view of itself, tall and square and pinkish-grey against a background of trees. (One form of architectural democracy would be for the great houses to be opened up visibly by vista to the public enlightenment.) And there is Knowlton Park, near small scattered Chillenden; its entrance facing a windmill on the bare down. It is not so generous with its charms as Goodnestone, affording only a glimpse, at the end of the long straight drive, of a central window and a great bunch of Tudor chimneys above it. In the church there is a memorial to the two sons of Sir John Narborough, who were drowned with their stepfather, Sir Cloudesley Shovel.

Between Eastry and Northbourne, there lies the coal-mining centre of Betteshanger, with its machinery lofted against the sky to divide the country from the sea. Considering their present importance—the Kentish miner produces on the average more and cheaper coal than any other—one would say that the Kentish coalfields are reasonably reticent. Tilmanstone, Northbourne, and Betteshanger itself have not the air of mining villages, and the countryside does not easily assume a carboniferous frown. It is a mercy, too, that if there must be coal-mining in Kent, it should be near the sea; for from the Betteshanger area the prospect of Deal is already a fever of vermilion roof-tops, and seaward there is not much for the mines to spoil. Eastward to Canterbury, however, terrible damage might be done to the scene if the mining spread widely.

Deal's sea-front has something of the good taste and effortless harmony of an old country town. The houses and pubs are of modest scale, simply designed in the eighteenth- or early nineteenth-century manner, and varying in pleasant tones of white, cream, and grey. They look over the Goodwins and the Downs (those which are in the sea), and the beach is shingly and somehow serviceable-looking—an affair of men who

Chilham Village

really know the sea. The Deal lifeboatmen rescuing victims of the Goodwins know it well enough.

Naturally the extremities of the front have not maintained traditional seemliness. The northern end goes badly to seed in the Victorian manner; and the southern, where the castle lies in some embarrassment at being overlooked by villas and terrace-houses, is not much better.

The castle is one of triplets—the others are Sandown and Walmer—begotten by Henry VIII on the plan of the Tudor rose; but his fortified system served a purpose he could hardly have foreseen when the castles were captured in the next century by Cromwell. Julius Caesar had less effect on our institutions than either of these strong men; but he is a greater historical figure, and Deal his probable landing place in Britain.

Deal's Georgian celebrity was Elizabeth Carter, born there in 1717 and educated by her father, a preacher of Canterbury Cathedral. He found her a bit slow, but nevertheless she became a queen bluestocking and, such was the tolerance of the age, a popular diner-out. Even Dr. Johnson was fond of her and approved of her intelligence; perhaps appeased by her ability to make a pudding or work a handkerchief. Her more remarkable achievements were her translation of Epictetus and her mastery of French, Italian, German, Spanish, Portuguese, and Arabic: and, needless to say, Latin and Greek.

Deal runs pleasantly enough into Walmer Green, and trees come down to frame the sea where the senior triplet stands. Walmer Castle is the official residence of the Lord Warden of the Cinque Ports—the present enviable sinecure-holder is Mr. Winston Churchill, of whom it might be said that he is the peer in prestige of his predecessor the Duke of Wellington. Most of the stories and the lares and penates are the Duke's, and you can see the camp-bed he used at Waterloo, the chair in which he died, and his reading-and-writing desk; as well as his boots (his name is preserved in boots, trees, and a great public school), a lock of his hair, and many other domestic belongings.

The plan of the castle is a series of circles and the resulting split-up of internal space is decidedly odd; but some of the rooms are charming, even when a slice of circle is lit only by one window in a wall twelve or thirteen feet thick. Queen Victoria's room is one such; but the Georgian additions are naturally the most elegant; the contribution of a Kentish Lord Warden, the Duke of Dorset from Knole. The furniture and decoration of the castle are for the most part simple and homely, and it is quite easy to imagine living there.

It was from here that the naval authorities watched Robert Fulton the American demonstrating his wonderful invention—the torpedo. Having failed to impress Napoleon, he now offered it with impartiality to the British. Unfortunately for him, they too turned it down, Trafalgar having made them quite content with naval warfare as it already was. The loser of that battle, Villeneuve, was entertained, rather than held captive, at Walmer, and allowed to go to London for Nelson's funeral. His reception in his own country, however, was less cordial, and he committed suicide at Rennes in 1806.

The cliffs rise steeper as you go south, and at Kingsdown and St. Margaret's Bay they are towering. On the top, St. Margaret-at-Cliffe seems to me a little sad and ghostly, like the Hoo villages, but it has a character of permanence much to be welcomed on a holiday coast. The Norman church was damaged in the second war by shell-fire from across the Channel.

At St. Margaret's Bay the nearness to France is underlined by precipitately sited houses called "Calais View" or "Gris Nez Villa"; and it is true that the French coast is visible from this part of ours, though not, apparently, when I am there. The little holiday settlement is reached from St. Margaret-at-Cliffe by a steep hairpin road on the thickly wooded cliff, and the surroundings have been likened to the Riviera. I would not go so far as that, but the little bay is certainly charming, and there is perhaps something un-English, and certainly un-Kentish, about the snugly-sited houses clinging to the chalk-face among the trees.

The approach to Dover is across the high Downland at cliff-top level; and the immediate introduction is a formidable technical installation presumably connected with Radar. It is too near the castle for visual comfort, and the outskirts of the famous town are of ordinary incoherence. We must ignore them.

I cannot write much of Dover's history: the key to England, the Roman city of Dubris, the chief of the Cinque Ports, the link with France and Europe. I can only try to give an impression of what it looks like to me. First of all, I like it very much better than Folkestone. It is by nature entirely unpretentious, and I doubt if many people would choose it for a holiday, except in the sense that holidays abroad emanate from it and the Lord Warden Hotel was, until the war stopped foreign travel and discouraged visitors to Dover, famous as the first refuge of honeymooners. From the Eastern Arm to Shakespeare Cliff the town has an air of purpose, and enough grace to redeem it from pure utilitarianism. Purpose has begotten charm in the inner harbour, where small establishments concerned with the traffic of the sea huddle against the background of cliffs; and of course the great harbour, with its lighthouse and Moles, is full of promise of adventure abroad.

I stayed there four years after the second war was over, when it was difficult to find room because most of the hotels and boarding-houses were ruinous and deserted. There was nothing of prosperity about the town; nor indeed very much of Regency grace in architecture except Waterloo Crescent, much of which has been sensibly restored and smartened into the White Cliffs Hotel; and those pleasant houses in the Eastern Arm which have not been closed by bombs and shell-fire. But what was left had soundness and simplicity, a modest decency and a sense of history which seems to be lacking in Folkestone. I came out of my Regency lodging and walked along the front past gaping windows in brown brick derelict façades; and felt that honour and pity and use were there, but not vulgarity.

What of the castle? I could not write a history of a stronghold rising, with a keep of Norman majesty, on earthworks dating from before the Roman occupation. But I can praise the fascinating Norman chapels, one above the other; so richly moulded, so masculine and calm; the vast banqueting halls with the names of French prisoners neatly carved on the walls; and the deep sense of security deriving from so many centuries of history and so much massiveness of structure. And I can record my awe as the guide dropped a lighted paraffin rag down the great well. This 400 feet fall of flame from the Keep to sea-level, lighting up the walls and diminishing in its descent into some

Barham Village

unimaginable Hell, is fascinating in the implications of horror. They show too what may once have been the keys of the castle, discovered by someone who braved the depths of the well; of a length suggesting a colossal thickness of door.

I suppose the garrison church of St. Mary de Castro might be thought as interesting as the castle by which it stands. It is said to have been built by Saxons out of Roman materials, and this is no doubt true. But I could detect very little Saxon feeling about the outside of the church—a great conundrum for anyone who has not read the guide-book. It could date from almost any time; but you are pretty sure it is an old church. Until you go in. Then you are confronted with large areas of tiles such as you might expect to find in some municipal baths—serviceable, durable, and damnable. They are, need I say it, the legacy of Sir Gilbert Scott.

He did not, however, "restore" the Pharos, or Roman lighthouse, which is separated from the church by no more than four or five feet; although I feel sure he would have knocked it into shape with the utmost confidence and gusto if he had had the chance. It really is a Roman building which, although more or less ruinous, yet rises higher than the nave of the church; the only thing left to us, I think, which is more than a fragment of that great building age.

The view from the castle is magnificent in spite of the fact that nowadays towns look worse from above than from their own level—the majority of roofs are raw or smarmy. Inland, the Downs rise into dramatic contours, and seaward the horizon seems immensely distant with France hidden in the haze.

In the town, the sights are not many: Hubert de Burgh's Maison Dieu, now a part of the Town Hall, with its beautiful exterior texture and fine range of painted windows, has another hall built on to it—Victorian with a faint Regency Gothick air and galleries like an early nineteenth-century church. Luckily this excrescence is on the side away from the charming Maison Dieu House, or Cloth Hall, which was built in 1665 for the Agent Victualler of the Navy; became a private house in William IV's reign; and is now the office of the Borough Surveyor; an exceptionally interesting design in red brick, with little tapering pilasters and entablatured dormers.

Of the two Norman churches, St. James's was almost entirely demolished by Nazi action, and St. Mary's, although a fine tower and doorway survive, is greatly spoiled by the additions of some misguided Victorian. The whole town has, at present, a rather endearing look of triumphant shabbiness.

Folkestone is entirely different; neither shabby nor triumphant, and not at all suggestive of its own history as an old port. It is a place for holidays, and its seaside social status is the highest in Kent. The lay-out is good: the Leas, the steep walks up the cliffs (or you can go by the little twin funicular), the nicely tended gardens. There are a few acceptable Early Victorian terraces at sea-level, and some older buildings in the harbour area. But on the whole, my impression is that here every form of architectural vulgarity has come into its own, and proudly at that. On the upper parade pomposity and tastelessness prosper unashamedly, and at the far western end expensive pretentiousness culminates in the Grand and Metropole Hotels.

From Folkestone, however, you can soon get into Downland country where views are grand and, by reason of some strangely contoured hills, even a little weird. Newington, a minute village almost on the London road, leads you up a tremendous slope into the Downs, from which views are beautiful and unblemished over a great punchbowl to the sea. At Paddlesworth you are 600 feet up in a remote yet affable countryside where views have to be sought between high hedges, and the sea makes their perfect background. Acrise has a great house deep in a park in well-wooded Downland; the Little Stour cuts a valley in the Downs for Elham with its manor house and old church; and Lyminge, too cluttered and elongated for high village honours, has a church whose original foundation was by St. Ethelburga in the seventh century.

Stowting, standing near the great Roman road which runs almost dead straight to Canterbury, is too small to compete for prizes, charming though it is; so I think one must choose between Postling and Brabourne for the best village in this part of the Downs. Postling Court, church, and half-timbered farm-buildings closing one side of the churchyard with an immensely long low roof—these form a delightful little group in a Downland hollow. The Court is romantic black and white of the Tudor age; the church mainly twelfth century: compact, neat, and of beautiful texture. Away to the east a great slanting clump of trees on an escarpment of the Downs emulates in profile the great West Sussex landmark of Chanctonbury Ring.

All the same, I think Brabourne is the better. The little group of buildings by the church is one of those instinctive and unconscious compositions which delight the eye as much as the thought-out schemes of the calculating architect. Nothing here is discordant, dolled-up, or crude. The church is largely Norman and has one or two rather exceptional points of interest: one is literal—the chancel-arch is not quite semi-circular, as if the builder had considered the possibilities of the pointed arch but hardly dared use it. Another is the little window on the north side of the altar, thought to be the oldest complete window in England, since the glass, as well as the opening, is Norman. There is, too, the shrine supposed to have held the heart of John Balliol, and the tombs and memorials of the Scotts of Scott's Hall, his descendants through Sir William Baliol le Scot. Twelve generations of the family lived at Scott's Hall, which was destroyed in 1808 and is now represented only by some crinkles in a field near the village of Smeeth.

Mersham is not far off, where the Knatchbulls owned from Henry VIII's time until lately the manor of Mersham-le-Hatch. The present house, built 1762–72, is the earliest complete country house by Robert Adam; a chaste and solid design in brick. Sir Wyndham Knatchbull specified that it should not be palatial but "kept entirely plain". He died at the age of twenty-six only a year after it was begun, and it was left to the elderly uncle who succeeded him to add the wings. The great architect thought that without them Mersham was too much like a town house, and the addition was certainly a great improvement.

The way back to the sea is through straggling Sellindge, birthplace of the mysterious Sir Edmund Berry Godfrey, whose murder was worked into the Popish Plot by Titus Oates. I will keep Hythe for my next section because it seems to belong to Romney Marsh; stopping for the moment at Sandgate. It has some Regency houses of comfortable mien on the sea front, and behind it a country-town High Street; so that although it is wedged and joined by Hythe and Folkestone its identity is separate and clear. On the hills above is the great conglomeration of Shorncliffe Camp, originally part of the defence scheme against Napoleonic invasion.

Carving on one of the capitals in the crypt of Canterbury Cathedral

5

Romney Marsh and Weald

THE Romans built the sea-wall at Dymchurch and other engineering works for reclaiming land from the sea. In their time much of the marsh was covered by it and is, of course, still below its level. But, just as Kent has lost ground at Hoo and Sheppey, so it has gained much even since Roman times. Recession and silting have left Sandwich, Lympne, Lydd, and New Romney well inland; and the island of Rye, over the Sussex border, is an island no longer.

The marsh is more or less crescent-shaped, full of ditches and channels, and, by reason of its geological history, extremely rich in pasture for sheep and cattle—sheep especially are famed, and their strain is to be found in flocks all over the world. These 45,000 acres, then, we owe to the Romans, and it is even said that Romney was called after Rome; but the Military Canal, which encloses the marsh from Hythe to Rye, and the many Martello towers which border it to seaward, are relics of the Napoleonic invasion which, like Hitler's, never came off.

Marshland, for me, is best for birds. I like the waders better than any others—snipe, redshank, woodcock, curlew, and sandpiper; and it is pleasant to know that the rare and graceful avocet, plumed in black and white, used once to nest on Romney Marsh. But I am not one who feels at home among great stretches of flat treeless fields and dykes; being properly appreciative only of the villages which rise, without help of contour, from their dubious foundations.

Hythe was once one of the Cinque Ports, but its harbour has silted and its glory been ravished by holiday amenities. From it the Romney, Hythe, and Dymchurch miniature railway, the world's smallest public line, runs to Dungeness. It was started as a private hobby, still delights the young of all ages, and will be maintained, one hopes, as evidence of English eccentricity and for the pleasure of children.

The old town has some solid virtues—the Town Hall is dignified late Georgian, and there is a mellow jumble in narrow streets; the great church, the vicarage and manor-house, and various remnants of a better building age, are good in themselves and isolated in the mind. But the general aspect of the place is untidy, muddled, and unattractive, and the gardens by the Military Canal are not such as I should care to sit in for long.

Dymchurch I know from family holidays there. It has managed to hang on to its village character in the face of appalling opposition; but I think it is weakening its hold. There is the Norman and Early English church; a few old houses of dignity and charm; and a sense of snugness behind the Roman wall. But there are also holiday camps, sites for caravans, and all the trappings of gregarious amusements which so unfortunately are enemies of beauty. One has to admit that the coast-line of Romney Marsh is more horribly blemished by shacks and shanties, from Hythe to Littlestone, than any part of the Kentish shore. I will say no more of it except that Dungeness, where the little railway ends, has a certain isolation of lighthouse, fishermen, and pub; and that its beach shelves so suddenly that shipping can find some protection here close in to the shore. Fishing is famed, bird-watchers have a fine field, and the few inhabitants negotiate the shingle shod with footboards.

Inland from the Dungeness desolation—the very name of Denge Marsh has a dismal sound—the two big villages or small towns of Lydd and New Romney appease the need for solidity of structure and firmness of ground. Both were once on the coast, Romney having been one of the Cinque Ports and the possessor of a priory, a hospital, and three churches. It still has a church with a 100-foot tower and some bits of the priory, but I think the best thing about it is the general character and colour of the High Street, full of Georgian good sense, comfort, and taste in creams and browns.

Lydd, which has all that too, is known for its church; the last and longest in the county, and sometimes rather obviously called "The Cathedral of the Marshes". In 1940

Dungeness

a bomb fell on it and wrecked the chancel, but when I was last there the work of restoration was in hand. It seems inapposite that this charming old place should have given its name to an explosive originally manufactured near by—Lyddite.

From New Romney two roads cross the marsh to the north-west; one running to Appledore on the Military Canal, the other to Ivychurch and so beyond the marsh to Ashford. I will join the Appledore road at Old Romney, a minute village which, too, once had a harbour. (New Romney took over that function and was then itself stranded by the recession of the sea.) Here is one of the most attractive of all the little marshland churches; beautifully visible from the village street as it sits in a field by old trees, with the great flats stretching away beyond. I think many people will agree with me that this sort of country is especially at the mercy of its buildings. When they are ramshackle or vulgar, there is no cover for their effrontery or their blushes; but when beautiful they benefit by and confer distinction on their plain setting.

Before the Brenzett cross-roads you should turn left, cross the railway-line, and come into Brookland village. It is difficult to remember all the old churches you have seen, and I think only mediaeval experts are proof against confusion and, eventually, boredom. But Brookland church is unforgettable because unique. You can't really say it is like Bexley or Upchurch, whose extinguisher spires I have already discussed. It beats them both for oddity, for although its extinguishers fit more comfortably than theirs they are much more strange for being three; because the lowest one reaches almost to the ground; and because the whole affair is a detached belfry.

The church itself is one of those which seem to be sinking into the marsh—it is surprising to me that worse has not happened to them in that soil. The columns of the aisles lean outwards from the great box-pews, and if the arch never sleeps it must be having a more than usually bad attack of insomnia at Brookland.

If you go through the village you cross Walland Marsh and are soon out of Kent; but back on the Romney–Appledore road you can find Brenzett, with its marsh church surrounded by trees, and, a mile or so eastward, Ivychurch, with another "Cathedral of the Marshes" by a pleasant inn. This overfit—it serves only a very small village—stands imposingly on what I think is the best part of the marsh: where the little road runs straight and clean and free from building to Newchurch. Here the outskirts of the village have been marred by new housing, but I shall not bewail that since almost anything new seems too insistent on the marsh. The centre of the village is delightful, and here again the church seems to be sinking, resignedly after so many centuries, into the rich earth.

I went from here back to the canal at Appledore by way of Snave and Snargate—I like the ugliness of their names—among channels and dykes across the great flat grazing grounds. Snargate church looks more uncomfortable than Brookland or Newchurch in its slow descent into the marsh. If its back isn't broken, it is decidedly bent, but it is imposing and venerable and much too big for its community.

As you approach the canal and the border of the marsh, the countryside takes on a more welcome and domesticated air. There are more trees than we have been used to, and the possibility of hills is felt, which I think is why all who are not marsh addicts like Appledore best of the Romney villages. Its name, of course, prejudices the ear in its

The road between Dungeness and Lydd

favour before any sight of it; like "Stone-cum-Ebony" not far off; and the broad street's proportions induce a sense of freedom. The old church, veiled by limes and standing near the canal to introduce the village to the marsh, has a wonderful diversity of window-design in the elevation to the road. No building in that pleasant street is worth a special mention, but I for one could live in Appledore more happily than anywhere else in the marsh.

The land keeps low in the Isle of Oxney, inland from the canal; where you can find Wittersham, whose fame is the discovery of an Iguanodon skeleton about ten million years old; or Smallhythe, where Ellen Terry's fifteenth-century half-timbered cottage belongs to the National Trust. Students of the drama can visit the museum here and see the relics of the great actress and of other famous stage figures including Mrs. Siddons; as well as the Priest's House and the barn-theatre.

The sea came round the Roman wall, circling up to Smallhythe round Oxney, so that until halfway through the fifteenth century Tenterden had Cinque Port privileges. It still has an air of distinction and prosperity in its broad High Street; and of a country town so happily sited that you can live right in it and yet have a fine view of the Weald. The wool trade flourished here and as usual induced much good building. The town is packed pretty tight with it, and the perpendicular church tower, with its corner pinnacles, crowns the ridge effectively. Celebrities are Caxton, accepted as born here, and Horatia Ward, the vicar's wife, whose fame it was to be the daughter of Nelson and Emma Hamilton.

We are at last getting into the Weald, which I take to be the essence of the vision of Kent. The word suggests, first of all, clay, which may not be good to live on, but which

I find much more beautiful, with its oaks and its brick and tile, than the Downland chalk, flint, and beech. Some parts of it, the Hastings Beds for instance, have gravel intermingled, and reach considerable heights in the Goudhurst ridge; providing a wonderful soil for fruit-growing and liable to break out into ironstone serrations—the Kent–Sussex border was the great iron-smelting area of England until the forests were depleted and iron was discovered in the north.

Coming from Tenterden by way of Woodchurch—a spacious village with a big green, a white windmill intact, and a pub called the "Bonny Cravat"—you sense a loss of richness in the land's aspect as you near the edge of the Weald at Ashford. I will not pretend to be very fond of the town. Its status as the centre of a railway system and works has spawned an industrial suburb, and even the ancient town-centre seems squashed in and confined. The church tower, pinnacled and silver-textured, looks well with half-timbered houses as a foreground; and also in a distant view; but the little square in which it stands is melancholy—some of the cottages are almost slummy and there seems little room to breathe at such close quarters to the church.

Sir Norton Knatchbull's Stuart Grammar School, not now used for its original purpose, is a nice little building, and the vicarage embraces bits of the college founded by Sir John Fogge, whose house survives, partially, in the square. He it was who rebuilt the church in the fifteenth century—the best of all, I think, for ecclesiastical architecture.

The south-eastern edge of the town has some good buildings, but in the market-place there are too many commercial indignities: one fine upper storey with a richly modillioned cornice is held up ignominiously on posts to the glory of the "Tailor of Taste".

Ashford's weekly market, deriving from the time of Edward I, is the rendezvous of Kentish farmers for the sale of sheep and cattle from Romney Marsh, as well as for a multitude of lesser trades.

There are the Knatchbulls of Mersham and the Smythe family, whose florid Elizabethan tombs have their own chapel in the church; and there is Jack Cade, the rebel peasant-leader of the fifteenth century. He does not seem to have had quite the necessary moral integrity for a striver against tyranny; having murdered a woman in Sussex, escaped to France, and fought against England before settling down as a doctor in Ashford. Like many modern proletarian leaders, too, he assumed a name, and it was as Mortimer, Captain of Kent, that he marched on London and sat down at Blackheath with 40,000 men. It all ended in a flop, and his forces faded away, leaving him to be killed on the way back to France. He was born an Irishman and so was not a genuine man of Kent.

Already at Great Chart the scene is wholly Wealden and the chalk forgotten. Hills are not high but continually give point to the views—more typically Kentish than any others—picturing clusters of white-cowled oasts and little churches on near horizons. The hop-gardens with their laden bines and the white weatherboarding of cottages, barns, and mills—these could hardly be anywhere else in the world than Kent. Here, in the spring, the men walk on stilts to set the strings on which the hops will grow; lured by "twiddling" with the hand.

Little Chart, whose church was wrecked by a flying-bomb, claims the oldest hop-garden in England; and Great Chart some intriguing brasses in its church: two men each

Hop pickers in the Weald

with five wives. William Sharpe died in 1499, and appears with the lot; and seventeenth-century Nicholas Toke, having taken five wives to his home at Godinton, set out on foot for London to look out for a sixth at the age of ninety-three.

The Toke family, in the person of Francis, is commemorated, too, in the charming Great Chart almshouses. Their inscription says that he founded them in 1582, and that they were rebuilt in 1833; for the homes of two aged people, who, if the conditions are complied with, must have plenty of room.

Of the excellent neighbouring Wealden villages, Bethersden, a warmly welcoming place, is known for the quarrying of a fossil-bearing marble or polishable limestone, of varying colours. Now, what is left of it is too crumbly to be worth getting out of Daniel's Water quarry. But it can be seen in both our cathedrals and in the towers of Tenterden and Biddenden, Smarden and Headcorn.

It may have been a matter for rejoicing over a victory won for aesthetics and the spirit that Tenterden tower was built of materials needed for the sea-wall bordering the Marsh. As a result, the sea broke through and covered much of the land, but the church, lofted on its little hill, proclaimed the supremacy of faith over works. I am not too sure I would have been on the side of the angels.

So many Weald villages have names ending in "den", that it is worth saying that the suffix implies a place cleared in the forest for the raising of hogs and other livestock. These "denes" were once the property of the King, when the Weald was a part of the great Forest of Anderida; but gradually it came to be accepted that other men had their rights, and the new owners often attached their own names to their denes, with such agreeable results as Bethersden, Smarden, Frittenden, and Tenterden.

I think High Halden has the sweetest aspect, by reason of its spacious sloping green, and its comfortable lay-out; and the unusual church tower, all wooden, square and octagonal, shingle-spired—this takes up the theme of restfulness and good sense.

But for individual buildings, Biddenden is perhaps best. Two of them are really beautiful seventeenth-century houses of moderate size, facing each other across the street; one with a square gazebo or garden-house. Round the corner, where the shops collect, there is much romantic half-timber work, including the Cloth Hall; and there is the church and a dilapidated windmill.

Biddenden has the horrid history of Eliza and Mary Chalkhurst, the Tudor Siamese Twins, whose birthplace it was. They bequeathed to the church a piece of land whose rent goes to charity and provides cheese, loaves, and cake, stamped with their double effigy. One version of the Biddenden Maids' story says that they died about 1570 at the age of twenty-seven, but that one might have survived if she had agreed to an operation after the other's death. But this is practically impossible to believe.

As you make for Goudhurst from Biddenden, you will see the little pyramid turrets of Sissinghurst Castle peering above the trees. I would say: miss almost anything in Kent rather than this. There is no need to miss it, since the gardens are open in the summer, and you can wander about them on your own. Most appropriately it is now the home of Mr. and Mrs. Harold Nicolson, both of them people of exceptional appreciation of art and history. Mrs. Nicolson is, of course, Victoria Sackville-West: poet, novelist, gardening expert, and daughter of Knole; and it was especially fitting that she should have rescued Sissinghurst from decay in 1930. For it was her ancestor Thomas Sackville, first Earl of Dorset, recipient of Knole from his cousin Queen Elizabeth, who married the daughter of Sir John Baker, builder of the castle around 1550.

Sir John held many grand offices under Henry VIII, Edward VI, and Mary: Chancellor of the Exchequer, Speaker of the House of Commons, Attorney General, and Recorder of London. But, to those who remember his career, he will always be "Bloody Baker". For Sissinghurst, named after a thirteenth-century lord of the manor, John de Saxenhurst, was built "on the blood and bones of English folk done to death by that human vulture Sir John Baker, Bloody Mary's Chancellor, who under the cloak of religious zeal won by torture and pillage sufficient wealth to build his palace".

These are the words of Mr. Richard Church, and few will think them too forceful. For there is a room over the south porch of Cranbrook church where Baker held Protestants for torture before sending them to be burnt alive.

One cannot help being disappointed that he himself died naturally, being succeeded by direct male descendants until 1730, when Sissinghurst was bought by Sir Horace Mann, well known for his indefatigable correspondence, from Florence, with Horace Walpole. He seems to have made no use of it except to let it to the government as a prison, for the incarceration of French prisoners during the Seven Years War. They were the last to see it in its entirety. One of their guards later achieved a greater distinction than any Baker, or even than Horace Walpole himself—Edward Gibbon, a young officer of militia.

In 1855 Castle House was built near the entrance and then inhabited by various farmers, but the castle mouldered away until its rescue by the present owners. There is not much left of it, yet it is one of the most beautiful places I know. My first visit was particularly fortunate, for on arrival by car I was immediately asked by a visitor awaiting his return: "Are you Mr. Nicolson?" Replying that I was not, but wished I were, I began my exploration in the best possible mood.

It is all really breath-takingly beautiful. The long low range of buildings screening the gatehouse is of the most velvety Tudor brickwork imaginable; full of small delightful puzzles for the antiquary—strange arches and surprising little brick-traceried windows round the entrance archway into the garden. The gatehouse, where V. Sackville-West writes, is placed on the skew to the arch. It doesn't matter why. Nor does it matter that it is absurdly high for its meagre width and stands isolated by the loss of the buildings which once tied it into the courtyard. The texture of the gatehouse and entrance range is so lovely that you think only of their present relationship to lawns and flowers. All is peace and even "Bloody Baker" doesn't matter. You go through the gatehouse on to the Tower Lawn, with the Priest's House on your left and the wonderful flower-garden on your right. In front is the yew walk, and beyond that the cottage and the orchard. There is the moat, and the nuttery, and the herb garden; and, at the extreme end of the grounds, a view of the rich Weald and of Frittenden church softened by distance into a happy silhouette.

The three estates of Angley, Bedgebury, and Glassenbury divide Cranbrook from Goudhurst with a terrain of dignified parkland and massy woods; rich in the sense of privilege although Angley House has gone, and Bedgebury is a girls' school. But Glassenbury is moated, fifteenth or sixteenth-century with some indiscretions of the nineteenth; guardian of the gravestone of Jaffa, Napoleon's charger, who died here aged thirty-eight.

The tradition and practice of hop and fruit-growing, weaving and smuggling; and the Kentish way of building in weatherboarding and painting it white, have made Cranbrook what it is. If you were dropped here by parachute through fog, you would know you were in Kent, simply because the old houses and the impressive church in yellowish stone and the magnificent windmill—the latter dated 1814, still working, and possibly the biggest and best in England—could be nowhere else.

The cloth-working industry derived from Edward III's invitation to the excellent Flemish weavers to become Kentish, and wherever these worthy people settled they left behind them things of good design and craftsmanship. They rebuilt the church and founded the school; and when Elizabeth was in Cranbrook she walked, they say, for three-quarters of a mile on native broadcloth laid down for the journey. A later celebrity was Daniel Defoe, who wrote *Robinson Crusoe* in an unidentified cottage near by. He was getting on for sixty when he produced his masterpiece.

If Cranbrook is for me the most typically Kentish of all our small towns, so are its countryside and views and contours the most unmistakable. The visual richness of soil, trees, and buildings continues right up to the Sussex border and well beyond it. Benenden is a village supremely spick and span—a carping investigator might wish for just a little dilapidation and dirt to soften its model cleanliness. The big green, honourable in cricket history, runs up to the great church—another magnificent overfit—and Hemsted Park, once Lord Cranbrook's home and now a school, marks the summit of the Weald of Kent at no more than 370 feet.

Rolvenden is long and spacious and unmistakably Kentish, on a ridge giving views to Tenterden in the east or little Newenden on the Sussex border—here marked by the Kent Ditch running along the side of Romney Marsh to the sea. Sandhurst and Hawkhurst are less well composed than the "Dens", but they have their place in the wealden picture, and Hawkhurst's Marlborough House School is a fine Georgian building.

Spring and early autumn are the times to be in a fruit-growing countryside, and it is difficult to be sure whether blossom or fruit is the more beautiful. But orchards are never, even in the bare interval of winter, without the promise of delight.

Lamberhurst was a centre of the iron industry and is now a pleasant village linking Scotney Castle, a mysterious compound of Plantagenet, Elizabethan, and later styles poised by a moat, with Bayham Abbey's romantically ruinous piers and arches: unconscious studies in the picturesque such as led astray the Georgian readers of "horrid" novels.

But Goudhurst at once suggests the common sense and good taste of the Flemish weavers who settled there. It is beautifully sited 400 feet up on a ridge commanding the Weald. It has been said that sixty-eight church towers or spires can be seen from here, but I think they would take some finding. Certainly the churchyard has a lovely view over the hopping and fruit country; dotted with the white cowls of the oasts and the poles delineating the hop-gardens.

It is said that the word "garden" applied to hops has its origin at Goudhurst, where a fourteenth-century vicar, whose stipend was paid in "lambs, wool, cows, calves, chickens, pigs, ducks, apples, pears, onions, and all other herbs sown in gardens", maintained that hops were included in this specification. He took his case to law against the Abbey of Leeds, and lost it; but time has made him the victor.

I like the yellow ragstone of the church, and the way some classic decoration, done during the Civil War, has settled down happily around the western door of a mediaeval building. Inside, the Culpeppers of Bedgebury are commemorated by some fine tombs—one shows father and mother and eighteen children at prayer; done with all the vigour and flamboyance in which the Elizabethans could indulge without trace of vulgarity. There are Culpeppers in the round and Culpeppers in the flat of brasses, for they were one of the great families of Kent—sixteen separate families, indeed, in Stuart times. That Thomas who was Catherine Howard's lover we have already encountered at Hollingbourne.

Although the best view is south from the church, round which the traditional smuggling centre, "The Star and Crown", and a row of weavers' houses cluster, you can look far in most directions from Goudhurst. But Mr. Church, who lives near the village, exactly matches my own feeling when he says he is not happy looking north, however loftily. North is barbarism, cold, and Calvinism; south the sun, the Mediterranean, "the

38. *A fine aerial view of Canterbury Cathedral showing how Bell Harry Tower dominates the city.* NEW YORK TIMES

39. *Canterbury Cathedral: the strength and aspiration of piers and vaulting.* DR. WEAVER

40. *Canterbury Cathedral: carving in the crypt.* WALTER SCOTT

41. *Maidstone: the magnificent fourteenth-century tithe-barn joins stone and half-timber delightfully.* A. F. KERSTING

42. *Maidstone: a view of the Medway showing the Archbishop's Palace and the church of All Saints.* HUMPHREY AND VERA JOEL

43. *Goudhurst village.* C. RIGHTON CAMPIN

44. *Mereworth Castle was designed by Colin Campbell, author of* Vitruvius Britannicus. *Campbell dispensed with chimney stacks by taking the flues up the ribs of the dome.* KENT MESSENGER

45. *Mereworth Castle : detail of doorway, frieze and cornice in the saloon, with a glimpse into the rotunda beneath the dome.* A. F. KERSTING

46. *Foot's Cray Place, like Mereworth Castle and Chiswick House, was architecturally inspired by Palladio's Villa Capra at Vicenza.* D. W. GARDNER

47. *Excellent village street architecture at Biddenden, famous for the Tudor Siamese twins Eliza and Mary Chalkhurst.* REECE WINSTONE

48. *Sissinghurst Castle exemplifies Tudor brickwork at its most beautiful. It was built by "Bloody Baker".* B. AND N. WESTWOOD

49. *Cranbrook is perhaps the best of all the Weavers' towns. The Flemish weavers invited to England by Edward III were everywhere excellent citizens and craftsmen. Cranbrook mill dates from 1814, and is probably the finest and biggest still working in England.* C. RIGHTON CAMPIN

50. *Smarden, a typical Wealden village with its weatherboarding and weather tiling.* LEONARD AND MARJORIE GAYTON

51. Left, *Staplehurst Church: hand wrought iron-work of the twelfth century. The ornaments may have been intended to act as charms against evil spirits.*
LEONARD AND MARJORIE GAYTON

52. Right, *Tenterden, a wool town with a fine broad High Street and a dominating fifteenth-century church tower. Horatia Ward, wife of a vicar of Tenterden, was the daughter of Nelson and Emma Hamilton.*

53. *Old Romney church in the marshland fields. A typical scene in a countryside famous for its sheep.* T. EDMONDSON

54. *Ashford church tower, silvery and pinnacled, dominates the countryside in which the town stands. The church was rebuilt in the Perpendicular period by Sir John Fogge, who also founded the college.* STANILAND PUGH

55. *Romney Marsh: the Royal Military Canal was a part of the defence scheme against invasion by Napoleon. It was planned so that a gun could command each section.* KENT MESSENGER

56. *Brookland church with its unique detached belfry. The church itself is one of those which seem, with infinite slowness, to be sinking into the marsh.*
LEONARD AND MARJORIE GAYTON

58. The mediaeval bridge over the Medway at Aylesford. It was said that Hengist and Horsa fought an important battle against the Britons on the site of the village.
LEONARD AND MARJORIE GAYTON

Opposite: 57. Old farmhouses at Elmstone Hole, near Grafty Green. LEONARD AND MARJORIE GAYTON

59. Ightham Mote: mediaeval romance in stone and half timber. Much of it dates from the fourteenth century.
COUNTRY LIFE

60. *General Wolfe, whose statue dominates the green at Westerham, was born at the vicarage, lived at Quebec House, and stayed at " The George and Dragon".* A. F. KERSTING

61. *Chevening was almost certainly designed by Inigo Jones, but its appearance has been entirely altered since his time. The first Lord Stanhope, Prime Minister in all but name, added the stables and library blocks, and the third, a scientist of radical tendencies, hid the main building behind yellow mathematical tiles.* COUNTRY LIFE

62. *Knole, one of the most famous and biggest houses in England, was built in the main by Archbishop Bourchier at the end of the fifteenth century, and remained an archiepiscopal palace till it was seized by Henry VIII. Queen Elizabeth gave it to her cousin Thomas Sackville, who married the daughter of "Bloody Baker" of Sissinghurst. It is now a National Trust property, but the descendants of Thomas Sackville still live there.* A. F. KERSTING

63. *Sevenoaks: Chantry House with its charming seventeenth-century façade, is perhaps the most interesting building in the old High Street.* NATIONAL BUILDINGS RECORD

64. Chiddingstone: the greater part of the village, including the Castle Inn, is National Trust property.

MUSTOGRAPH

65. Cottages at Nizels Weald, near Sevenoaks.

C. RIGHTON CAMPIN

66. *Penshurst: the church is built of yellowish stone which has weathered into harmony with the surrounding brick, plaster, and half timber.* HUMPHREY AND VERA JOEL

67. *Oasthouses at Penshurst—the most typical element of Kentish scenery.* TRAVEL ASSOCIATION

68. *Penshurst Place : a pattern of plates.* NATIONAL BUILDINGS RECORD

69. *Penshurst Place : the home of Sir Philip Sidney, forms part of Kent's best composition of great house, church, park, and village.* KENT MESSENGER

70. *Tunbridge Wells: the Pantiles, once the promenade of fashion and frivolity, has still an air and some buildings of great charm.* CROWN COPYRIGHT

71. *Tunbridge Wells: the seventeenth-century church of King Charles the Martyr with its remarkable plaster ceiling.* A. F. KERSTING

72. Calverley Crescent, in Tunbridge Wells, was originally designed by Decimus Burton as a parade of shops with lodgings above.

REECE WINSTONE

73. The cricket ball industry flourishes in the neighbourhood of Tonbridge and Maidstone. Mr. H. Martin is seen weighing the balls at a factory established in 1808.

FOX PHOTOS

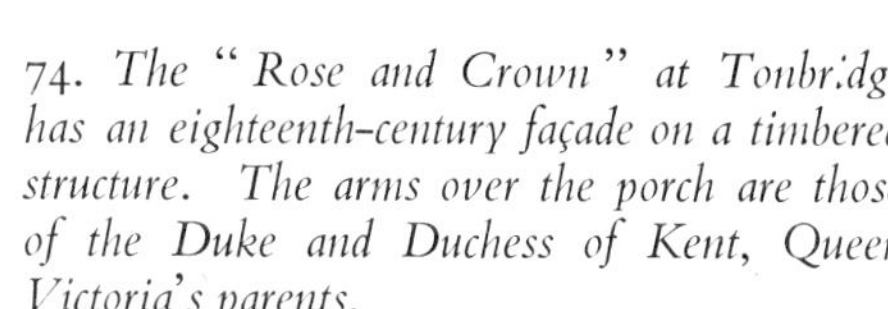

74. The "Rose and Crown" at Tonbridge has an eighteenth-century façade on a timbered structure. The arms over the porch are those of the Duke and Duchess of Kent, Queen Victoria's parents.

NATIONAL BUILDINGS RECORD

centre of civilisation and right living, and the wines of France". It may have been the Calvinistic spirit which changed the charmingly named Courtesan Green, where Mr. Church thinks one of the Lords of Glassenbury had established a mistress, into Curtisden Green. I wish she could be nominally reinstated.

Frittenden, whose church we saw from Sissinghurst, is a nice little hidden village, and Headcorn has breadth of street and a cloth-worker's hall and a thirteenth-century bridge over the little river Beult. The stout church-tower rises from the willow-fringed water-meadows, and the railway runs by without leaving unseemly evidence or taking roots as it pauses on the way to the coast.

Deeper into the Weald again, back through the unspectacular Staplehurst and Marden, you come to the Teise, an obscure little Kentish river flowing between Horsmonden and Goudhurst to the Sussex border. Considerable hills stand about the valley, and on one of them stands the rather pathetic "Folly" of Scott's Tower.

It is quite without the frivolity of more expensive ventures into the picturesque, and looks likely to disintegrate—already a jagged-toothed cavern of stuccoed brickwork proclaims a partial collapse. But I think it is worth preserving for the idea which gave it form: not the debased form of more ambitious follies, but the forlorn simplicity of a small smooth swollen cylinder with a staircase turret and no decoration to relieve or deepen its melancholy.

The idea and the pathos derive from its building by the rector of Horsmonden, presumably soon after the death in 1832 of Sir Walter Scott. This personal tribute is all the sadder in that its expression is so meagre. Follies, if they are to be foolish on the grand scale, cost a lot of money, and this the rector of Horsmonden probably lacked. But he did his best to honour the man he admired, and what writer would not be grateful for such homage as this? Horsmonden church and rectory are by the Teise about two miles from the village; west of them rises a smooth-contoured hill; and on top of this, easily seen from the road, is Scott's Tower.

I was lucky enough to be there when the great views were fading into dusk; and still luckier to witness a thunderstorm crackling around in honour of the great romantic novelist. It was not ghostly or oppressive; but sad, so sad; expressing for me the humble pride of the rector, and his hero's well-meaning championship of the Romantic Movement. I left Scott's Tower to a storm and deluge full of those off-stage dramatic effects which were its proper setting.

Expressive of the precisely opposite spirit—in which I find myself much more at home—is the supremely gracious Finchcocks, standing in a park in the unspoiled valley of the Teise; about equidistant from Scott's Tower and Scotney Castle. Where they are romantic and savage in spirit—even if the savagery of 1832 is somewhat synthetic—it is of the essence of humanism and enlightenment; built by the Bathursts in the early eighteenth-century, when men rejoiced at their liberation from irrational fears, and it was not yet thought amusing to dabble in picturesque voodoo. The Georgians followed the classic ideal of grace, repose, and order; and so sweet was their taste that what might have been merely mathematical was almost always endowed with charm. Finchcocks has that and magnificence too. It is probably the finest house of that period in Kent.

A little to the south, Kilndown has two interesting things: a Gothic Revival church

Brenchley

of Lancet instead of the more usual "Middle Pointed" design; and an inn of a sign which I have not seen elsewhere—"The Globe and Rainbow". But Brenchley is too full of good things to be dependent on such intellectual or literary details. It lies on a high undulation of the Weald north-west of Horsmonden; a mass of half-timbering, brick, stone, and painted stucco all miraculously harmonising in a haphazard layout. Matfield Green I find even better because I like a broad flat green without traffic on three sides better than a village street hedged about even with buildings of the best. Here you could live in a village and yet spaciously and quietly. The road runs by, passing a new housing scheme skilfully sited and designed, leaving the great green to its fine Georgian house, with its seventeenth-century turreted stable-block, in command of the scene. There are old cottages sparsely spaced; an early Victorian villa veiled in a bright garden; weather-boarded cottages and an excellent inn on the green's edge. This is a place to live in.

I have reached my chosen boundary, and so must go north to Paddock Wood, continuing among the orchards and hop-gardens to where the Beult runs by Hunton and through Yalding to join the Medway; into that country where the true Weald gives place to the Maidstone Ridge.

I was at Yalding in the hopping season when, I am afraid, villages do not appear at their best. Hopping is an insistent element in the Kentish picture, but although the permanent evidence—the gardens and oasts—is the greatest enrichment of the landscape, the short-lived human activity to which it works up results in a good deal of litter and squalor. The great green at Yalding accepts a vast concourse of caravans and shacks and primitive vehicles; a medley of strange invaders from London with a variegated smattering of gypsies. It accepts them because of their essential function in its economy; but the vision of the village is marred by their presence. Only in the hop-gardens do the hoppers come pictorially into their own. There, almost any arrangement of colour in shirt and skirt makes a pleasant harmony among the poles; and the groups of men, women, and children seen against the tall bines ask to be painted rather than verbally described.

I keep thinking: here is where I would live; and then, no, here. But Yalding is certainly high on my list. It has that tremendous green—not a true village green because it is not the centre of the village; its lovely old stone bridges across the Beult; a lock, and some small riverside appointments. All this besides the major excellencies of the village itself. There is the church, whose square tower has a circular turret growing out of it and culminates in a spiked onion-dome. There is the broad street where stands, by the church, a fine eighteenth-century vicarage; and, a little farther up, an unusual seventeenth-century design in admirable brick, generously pedimented. A butcher's shop stands actually on the old stone bridge spanning the stream, and outside the village there is a half-timbered house whose garden is full of architectural topiary-work.

I went on to Hunton, where the Court is a simple classical mansion in a park remarkably rich in Wellingtonias—the lake makes, however, a much more attractive foreground. It was the home of Sir Henry Campbell-Bannerman, whose rather uninteresting plaque in the little church is entirely overshadowed by the monuments of the Fane family; and outdone in fame by the old glass, once in Canterbury Cathedral, displaying the royal arms and also those of that almost enviable wife of Henry VIII—Catherine Parr.

Campbell-Bannerman is, I think, the most under-estimated of English Prime Ministers. Without his humane and enlightened South African policy the history of our times might well have been even worse than it is. He was that most typical and best of Englishmen—the man who governs because he believes he ought to, but gets away from government as often as he decently can. It might not be too much to say that only those men are fit to rule who rule reluctantly.

Church of St. Thomas à Becket, Fairfield

6

Kentish Hills; Surrey and Sussex Borders

IF Tunbridge Wells is disappointing, that is no doubt because Bath, Buxton, and Leamington have led one to expect so much in the way of architectural amenities from any place where English fashion (and to a lesser extent ill health) has been wont to take the waters. The beneficial chalybeate spring, discovered as early as 1606 by Lord North and still bubbling in the Pantiles, does not seem to have induced very much magnificence of décor; but the Wells retained its vogue up till Victorian times, although it was by then already eclipsed by the splendour of Brighton and the solace of sea-water.

But we are concerned with its glorious past, and its present which must await posterity's gift of an adjective. Lord North was the tutor of that Prince Henry whose death, involving the succession of Charles I, so profoundly influences our lives, one may suppose, even today. Henrietta Maria, Queen by reason of the young man's death, came to Tunbridge Wells with a great concourse—such was the legend of the spring that devotees had to camp out on the surrounding hills. There came also, at a later date, Catherine of Braganza, the plain Portuguese Queen of Charles II; one of those unfortunate women who, childless, had to bear the knowledge of a husband's fertility through other unions.

Royal patronage of any sort, however, was just what the place needed, and it was not long before the Pantiles became the promenade for all the smart foolery and vice of a profligate society with a medical excuse. The infamous Lord Rochester, Restoration rake, was there to write a poem on the frivolity and corruption of the trifling throng—he who was called by Hume "a plague spot of English literature". I cannot agree with that criticism. Of English morals, perhaps, but not of a literature to which he contributed:

> Love—the most generous passion of the mind:
> The softest refuge innocence can find;

calling it also:

> That cordial drop Heav'n in our Cup has thrown,
> To make the nauseous draft of life go down.

I had better not start on quacks; on Dr. Rowzee and Dr. Madan; for I am one of those illogical sceptics who can never believe in the healing properties of any waters. But of course I am interested in the people who, for one reason or another, took them at Tunbridge Wells: Samuel Richardson the founder of the English novel; David Garrick, Beau Nash, and the bluestockings Elizabeth Montague and Elizabeth Carter.

What of the present aspect of the place? Its virtues, I think, consist of Mount Ephraim, the Pantiles, and Calverley Park; places which still have something of the message of the spa even though their air is now respectable rather than fashionable. Mount Ephraim is a hill sprouting great sandstone rocks; very much in the picturesque Regency taste; with some tastefully sad-looking hotels and villas—the Mount Ephraim Hotel is charming, with a great lion and unicorn surmounting it.

Down the hill, too, there are more pleasant houses and hotels; and, tucked away at the bottom, the Pantiles; still delightful as a small enclosed parade hedged about with old buildings; lofted above the street where the old Assembly Rooms have become the Pantechnicon furniture-store and the statue stands on the Corn Exchange parapet.

The Pantiles—originally called "The Walks" and later "The Parade"—has suffered some elevational indignities at first and second floor level, but much still pleases—lime trees border one side, and a colonnade the other. The shops and restaurants behind the slender columns are for the most part well designed and inviting; and opposite is an excellent old grocer's shop, the little disused Georgian Music Gallery, and some other pleasant survivals of the ages of taste. The building which houses the chalybeate spring stands at one end, architecturally dubious; the modern and virtueless bandstand in the middle; and the vista is closed by the ugly Pump Room, long divorced from its proper purpose. Certainly one can say that few towns have any place so pleasant as the Pantiles for drinking beer or coffee and listening to music in the open air.

Calverley Park has the distinction of being the work of the great builder James Burton and his tenth son Decimus—that stately architect. Not all the houses are quite worthy of him, but the general effect is dignified and tasteful, although in some cases the yellow stone has turned to a depressing grey. The lay-out is informal; the gardens inviting with cedars and lawns; and if one were to live in Tunbridge Wells, Calverley Park would be first choice.

Just outside the park, Calverley Crescent is formal and urban; a system of terrace houses reduced to their lowest terms by Decimus. It is almost too austere and tenuous, rebuking the later flamboyance and vulgarity of design with something of the self-conscious virtue which the modernists affect. The answer to this puzzle is that the crescent was originally a parade of shops which filled in the meagre colonnade, the upper storeys being used as lodgings.

For the rest, you can find pleasant little corners and small groups of interesting houses if you look carefully, especially in the district of Mount Sion. (It is said that these Mounts, Ephraim and Sion, were so christened by Cromwellian soldiers; but that can hardly apply to Mount Pleasant and Mount Edgecumbe.)

Churches are very unorthodox: Holy Trinity, where Decimus Burton's Gothic is shown to be infinitely better than that of the Victorian experts; King Charles the Martyr, a seventeenth-century church with an amazing plaster ceiling but almost entirely rebuilt externally; the Doric temple on Mount Pleasant which is Congregational; and the Catholic church of St. Augustine, whose classic severity is insulted by a deplorable tower.

Round the town, hills are quite unlike the chalk Downs; thickly wooded, discontinuous, and rocky; extending east and west, and southward beyond the Sussex border. This makes a loop to contain in our county Ashurst and Groombridge Place—Groombridge village, with its steep green crowned with old cottages, and its rare church in seventeenth-century brick, is in Sussex.

Ashurst is somewhat amorphous, but its little white-turreted church and the lands

The Medway

of Ashurst Park are attractive near the source of the Medway. Here, however, you sense the nearness of a town as you do not at Groombridge, whose great house is very probably by Wren. The moat tells you that a much older one was here; in it Sir Richard Waller held as hostage John of Orleans, after rescuing his father Charles from the field of Agincourt.

The entrance to Groombridge Place, by a lake with a swan, is in the village; but there is a footpath by the church, leading across the park and drive and affording an excellent view of the house. On the central axis there is a range of Wellingtonias which seem too foreign to frame such an English picture as this. Absolutely English it is; but not, in my opinion, a very interesting design from the master-architect's drawing-board.

We must go back north, now, in order to stay in Kent; branching off the Tunbridge Wells road on the way to Penshurst by way of Speldhurst and Bidborough. Of these two the first is incoherent and has nothing much for praise—Gothic Revivalists might be interested in a pseudo-Early English church; and Bidborough's fame is to be a part of the Sidney legend; for Lady Dorothy, to whom another Waller wrote "Go, lovely Rose!" lived at Great Bounds, an estate which has disintegrated.

Penshurst is much more than the home of the legend; it is perhaps Kent's happiest entity of great house, park, and village. Everything composes perfectly. Church and vicarage, both beautiful, stand together near the great house, and the entrance to the churchyard is through a romantic archway formed by the joining of timbered houses. (There is a good deal of sham Tudor building in the village, and the visitor may be foxed, since the deception is more than usually skilful.)

Opposite the vicarage, the "Leicester Arms" is an excellent country hotel; several distinguished houses honour the village; there is a bridge over the young Medway; and all around a friendly landscape of parkland, little hills, and noble trees.

Sir Philip Sidney touches the imagination somewhat in the manner of Lord Falkland, victim of both sides in the Civil War; but he must have been a far happier hero, not torn by any conflict of loyalties and beliefs, although it seems that his Queen failed properly to appreciate him. For both were what all men in their hearts would like to be: poets and scholars and men of action in one; famous, yet honourable and modest; men who shone in the light of their own times and will never be forgotten.

Philip was born at Penshurst in 1559, the son of Sir Henry Sidney and grandson of that Sir William, Knight Banneret, to whom Edward VI gave the "House of Pencester with the Mannors, Landes and Appurtenances thereunto belonginge." These words are inscribed on the King's Gate which is the entrance to the great house. Sir Henry had already built the north and west fronts on to the original mediaeval house when, in 1585, he set up the King's Gate.

The great hall is the finest in England—built about 1340 by Sir John de Pulteney, four times Lord Mayor of London; its pleasant goldish stone blending happily with the Elizabethan brickwork of Sir Henry's courtyard.

Another part of this court is of the early nineteenth century, but accords well with what it adjoins since the architect made no attempt to be amusing. He was a son of Biagio Rebecca, the Italian painter who so often and so wonderfully collaborated with James Wyatt and "Capability" Brown.

The vision of Penshurst is far less clearly focused than Knole's. Where Knole approaches the precision of the Renaissance, Penshurst has some of the haphazardry of long slow growth—not too much, as I think Ightham Mote has, but enough to make it far more personal in charm than the great palace of the Sackvilles. Inside, despite the magnificence of pictures, furniture, and decoration, there is a deep sense of warm liveability. It is essentially a home.

Of pictures, apart from those of Sir Philip, one best remembers Colonel Algernon Sidney, executed for his supposed share in the Rye House Plot against Charles II. One version of the story has him sentenced on treacherous evidence by the sadistic Judge Jeffreys, and Lord John Russell thought it was a case of the foul murder of a gallant gentleman. But what I heard at Penshurst was that Algernon was a bad lot who gave his word to the King not to work against him; was allowed back from exile on that condition; and promptly broke his promise. The pictures of him as a child and young man certainly suggest that he might be capable of any villainy; but the Sidney family, basking in the permanent sunshine of Philip's reputation, can surely afford one villain in their history.

I found most appealing the picture of Charles I's little daughter Elizabeth, who spent some time after the regicide in the care of Lord and Lady Leicester at Penshurst. (Philip's brother Robert had been created an earl in 1618.) She was reasonably happy there, but the Parliamentarians insisted on her removal to Carisbrooke, where she died a month later of a broken heart. How dreadful is political fanaticism.

It was interesting to hear that one of the Sidneys, as Master of the Ordnance, for the sake of honesty and efficiency instituted the present system of inspection by stamping pieces of ordnance with his own crest; and that the arrow which we now see on government stores is derived from the Sidney chevron.

The earldom of Leicester died out in 1743, and Penshurst went to the daughters of Colonel Thomas Sidney. One of them, Elizabeth, became the wife of William Perry, and their daughter married Sir Bysshe Shelley, thus linking two immortal names in the person of their son, John Shelley-Sidney, uncle of the poet.

His son was created Lord de L'Isle and Dudley in 1835, and the present holder of that title, the owner of Penshurst, carried on the tradition of gallantry by winning the V.C. in the second world war. Thus are Zutphen and North Africa joined in the history of the Sidneys.

Leigh—pronounced Lie, like the prevalent surname in my village—has a pleasant green where cricket is played. But it cannot compare, as a village, with Penshurst. The bogus half-timbering of cottages, much of it built with the best intentions by Samuel Morley, the commercial philanthropist of Hall Place near by, is a little too suggestive of rustic musical comedy scenery. But the setting is altogether delightful.

Here I turn westward, leaving Tonbridge for later, and come to Chiddingstone Causeway, whose street runs parallel with that terrific straight line of railway from Ashford into Surrey. The green is wedged in between the railway embankment and the road, so that batsmen fond of hitting sixes must be absolutely dreaded by the fielding side. It is not a very memorable village, and of its buildings I shall confine myself to two. At the church of St. Luke, Bentley showed that the Gothic Revival, however regrettable, could at a pinch generate a pleasant little village church. (He was the architect of the colossal Byzantine Westminster Cathedral.) And, at the other end of the village, the honourable firm of John Wisden proves that a new factory need not ruin an old village. The Tonbridge area has a traditional industry for the making of cricket bats, balls, and other equipment; and this factory, while not pretending to look like a row of cottages, preserves the local building tradition in weather-tiles and pitched roof.

Chiddingstone itself is a mile or two away on the other side of the railway; a National Trust property consisting of a little street of half-timbered cottages, the "Castle", and the mainly thirteenth-century church. The castle itself was rebuilt at the end of the seventeenth century by the Streatfeilds of that time—their descendants are still a dominant family in this part of Kent. In the park, the Chiding Stone is a vast lump of sandstone about which certain improbable Druidic legends have grown up.

At Bough Beech, prettily named, the great railway line runs deeply through the village and yet seems not to spoil its character. The bridge over it is so narrow and inconspicuous that one might expect it to span nothing more than a stream, and buildings are mostly old weather-tiled cottages.

Hever village is even smaller, snug and secret in this little weald. There is the broach-spired church, of beautifully textured ragstone, standing by the Castle entrance; the Henry VIII Inn, reconstructed in the style of his time; and the essential brick and weather-tiling of cottages. In the church is a brass of Sir Thomas Boleyn, owner of the castle where Anne was born. Henry, that voracious house-grabber, seized Hever from Sir Thomas after murdering his daughter; and, as if to show his thoroughness in any project, also sent Anne's brother to the block. Naturally the Boleyn story dominates Hever, but the Castle was there in the days of Richard II and owes much of its present aspect to the enlightened American millionaire Lord Astor, and to Colonel J. J. Astor of *The Times*. It was, indeed, Lord Astor who made the marvellous eighteen-acre lake and the Italian gardens which really do make it possible, on some occasions and in certain lights, to imagine yourself in Italy. The Astor additions to the castle, although in half-timber, must be called successful, but I think romanticism is rather over-emphasised by the creepers which cover so much of the main building. This is, of course, intentional, since no old castle is better preserved and tended, but I happen to have a great dislike of riotous vegetation obscuring good design and materials.

This countryside is curiously secretive; it is not enclosed by high banks or sudden hills, and there are near views of the ragstone ridge; but these seem to be got by peeping—the landscape never opens up and the lanes have the suggestion of reluctance to lead anywhere. It is wealden in richness of oak and clay, but it is not the true fruit and hop-growing Weald. There are orchards and plenty of oasts, but the fruit trees are not in broad and serried masses and the kilns are often used for purposes other than the drying of hops. Farms are many, and their outbuildings, as always except when science and lack of timber have brought great concrete barns, grow out of and adorn the landscape. There is a small riverside, where the Eden flows by Hever and Chiddingstone to join the Medway at Penshurst; but this, too, is without the Arcadian glamour of Oxfordshire or Berkshire streams; modest and inconspicuous, like all the little weald.

At Cowden, a typical village of the old Kent and Sussex iron industry, you are almost on the county border. It is full of my favourite white weatherboarding, with which the inn admirably conforms, in an attractively devious little street. From here we can only go north to Edenbridge, which I think of as the capital of the little weald. The long street is bridged by the sign-board of "The Crown"; agreeably non-committal in architecture, and giving place to a bridge over the Eden, whose meadows are overlooked by the stout church. Hereabouts, where the river rambles in deepish banks, one sees the biggest firework show in England after much ribaldry of procession and pageantry through the town. To me, however, the essence of Edenbridge is the smell, pervasive but not unpleasant, of the tannery which carries on a country-town industry there.

My chief association with Four Elms, too, is somewhat unpoetic: walking down the lane one summer morning, I was suddenly confronted with two elephants, whose presence was easily explained, but not on the immediate sight of them, by the visit of a circus to Edenbridge. Four Elms has, besides the expected prettiness of this countryside, one of the finest village cricket grounds I know.

My scheme involves a move eastward here, back through Bough Beech, branching off at Chiddingstone Causeway, and bringing me out on the main road between Sevenoaks and Tonbridge at Hildenborough. Its position on the traffic artery has spoiled a place which was never meant to be more than a hamlet; and Hildenborough is now shapeless and conglomerate. A few Georgian cottages try to stress the old village centre, but the church is Victorian Gothic Revival of the Lancet phase. Probably the most interesting thing about the place is a housing scheme by the Hilden Brook, new at the time of writing; well designed and laid out, but naturally not conducive to a sense of rurality. And Hilden Manor, where the young and gay can dance, drink, or bathe, is a charming old house—perhaps a bit disapproving of its own swimming-pool and regretful of its lost acres.

School and Castle dominate Tonbridge, and the Medway cuts it into halves of which the northern is, on the whole, old and good, and the southern young and bad. Scholastic buildings are the introduction to the town from Sevenoaks, and they are an interesting collection, although none survive from the original foundation by Sir Andrew Judd, Elizabethan Member of the Skinners' Company.

Victorian collegiate architecture is usually depressing in the extreme, but the main buildings of Tonbridge are without the awful gloom of Scott and Waterhouse at Oxford and Cambridge. They have the advantage of the yellow ragstone, which weathers well, and the detail is sensibly simple. The great entrance quadrangle incorporates the oldest part of the school to be used as such—the Library—built in 1760 and enlarged in 1826—and there is a piece of Gothicised Georgian in the southern range. The old chapel, detached in the foreground, is now the School Museum and remarkably good for its date, which is 1859. It seems quite happy beside Judd House, the fine Georgian building which was taken over by the school in 1827, and one must be grateful to the various obscure architects employed at Tonbridge: E. H. Burnell, Campbell Jones, and the firm of Wadmore and Baker. They seem to have had no intention of insulting the dignity of Judd House and Ferox Hall—another Georgian Mansion belonging to the school on the opposite side of the street. The vast school Chapel, although obviously the later work of an intelligent architect, is rather red and raw in contrast with the stone. Luckily it does not come into the main view of the school from the road.

The castle is at the other end of the old High Street, lofted on its mound above the Medway. Nothing much is left except the thirteenth-century gatehouse built of the same yellow ashlar as the school; but in 1793 an excellent house now used as Council Offices was built on to it and a most happy marriage between mediaeval and classical was solemnised.

Tonbridge's most important hotel, the "Rose and Crown", is an old building with a fine Georgian façade and a porch surmounted by the arms of the Duke and Duchess of Kent—parents of Queen Victoria. Tradition pleasantly links the inn with the school, for on the last Wednesday in July the Master of the Skinners' Company comes out on to the balcony over the porch to represent the Governors and receive the acclamations of the boys. The great Tom Pawley, for twenty-five years secretary of the Kent Cricket Club, was landlord here, and of course Tonbridge is as redolent of cricket as anywhere in our profoundly cricket-minded county. It is the centre of the bat and ball making industry; John Wisden carries on his honourable work in the town; and the famous Frank Woolley, possibly the most beautiful artist of batsmanship the world has ever seen, started his cricket-school here.

Of mediaeval buildings there are the "Chequers", the "Portreve's House", and Aplin's restaurant—all probably of the fifteenth century; and the parish church of St. Peter and St. Paul; but the main aspect of the town is eighteenth and early nineteenth century. There is plenty of good building of that time in brick and weatherboarding, and a richness of names: Bordyke, Little Fish Hall and Great Fish Hall, the Hectorage, Potkiln Cottages, Starvecrow House, and Streamlands.

In Lodge Oak Lane, too, there is a small seventeenth-century pub delightfully called "The Cardinal's Error". It is for me a new sign, and may indeed be newly invented, for until lately the place was a cottage called Lodge Oak.

Tonbridge Castle

The Hadlow road leads you eastward, with a surprisingly quick change of scenery, straight into the real hop-garden country of the northern Weald. It is open and smiling and uniquely landmarked by the tower of Hadlow Castle, which I hope may always be preserved for its—what? Architectural value? Hardly. Sentimental interest? I doubt it. No. It is valuable simply for its pictorial quality; really beautiful in silhouette as it rises from the flat hop and fruit lands.

But only students of Folly should look closely at it; for, alas, its shape is its only virtue: the meretriciousness of gingerbread material and detail is all too obvious; and even the pretty little glimpse of it from near by in the village is best kept out of focus. The rest of the house is appallingly bad Gothick, pretentious and gimcrack, not to be regretted if it moulders to collapse. In the long and dismal hall, in the livid light of the stained-glass staircase-window, I saw white marble standing figures; one with a gin-bottle under its arm and one wearing a gas-mask.

The Peckhams, East and West, hardly seem related to each other: East much the bigger, rambling among hop-gardens, West more of the ragstone ridge, intimate and secluded by a green, with a beautiful seventeenth-century house in velvety brickwork among superb yews. And Beltring has nothing much but a great bunch of oasts, the biggest I remember; about twenty-six of them in a composition which wants to be painted rather than described.

Mereworth is away to the north, on the very edge of the hop-country; dominated, like Hadlow, by a piece of architectural individualism. The church must arrest the visitor who ordinarily doesn't bother with churches; but he probably won't like it: the tower and spire consist of an unusual arrangement of Renaissance motifs in yellowish stone, and the west end has an order of columns and great overhanging eaves more or less in the Tuscan manner of St. Paul's, Covent Garden—very much an architect's church. It was built by the Georgian Lord Westmoreland to replace an old one whose destruction was involved in the layout of Mereworth Castle.

Castle! No word could be more inapposite. We have already been to Foot's Cray Place and found a domed Palladian villa with four porticos. Mereworth is a finer version of that; designed by Colin Campbell, the author of *Vitruvius Britannicus*, a devoted Palladian; and built in 1723, four years before Lord Burlington's equivalent at Chiswick. It is the sort of place most disapproved of by mediaevalists and modernists: too cold and mathematical for romantics and too inertly aristocratic for the mystics of engineering and sociology. I doubt if Campbell's ingenuity in taking up the flues in the ribs of the dome to discharge their smoke through the lantern would appeal much to the worshippers of Le Corbusier.

But for Georgian enthusiasts there is much delight in this formality of great villa flanked by stable-blocks; approached by an avenue which disappears between lodges on the other side of the road. Even Horace Walpole, already seduced by the Romantic Movement, wrote in 1752 that Mereworth was "so perfect in the Palladian taste that I must own it has recovered me a little from Gothic". He disapproved of the flues, however, and also, more surprisingly, of the church.

Inside, the magnificence is restrained to liveability, and only the great drawing-room's magnificent decoration is perhaps a little overpowering. The rotunda beneath the dome is tremendously impressive, and the only thing I should not like about living at Mereworth would be the vertigo induced by looking down into it from the gallery.

Between here and Maidstone there are Wateringbury, old and mellow near the Medway; Teston, with an old bridge over the river and an honourable abolitionist tradition involving Admiral Middleton of Barham Court; and the nondescript village of East Barming. After that, the suburbs of Maidstone.

One must admit that the county town of Kent is not very encouraging to the sightseer. For one thing, there seems always to be a jam of traffic bound for the sea; for another, the view down the Medway displays a really horrible jumble of industrial detritus which includes the manifestations of the gas industry—always difficult, if not impossible, for a town to absorb happily. Beyond all this ugliness, the barges come tranquilly up the river from Rochester.

But if you can get away from the exhaust fumes in the High Street, you may detect the much more agreeable smell of malt from the great breweries. Brewing is one of those industries which only cranks deplore, and its buildings are often seemly. Certainly it is appropriate to a county so intimately connected with the growing of hops.

Up river, the view from the bridge is peaceful with punts lying near the Old Palace,

Hadlow Village

Oasthouses near Maidstone

which rises beautifully above the river and composes with the great Perpendicular church of All Saints—surely one of the finest in Kent (the same old story belongs here—Henry VIII grabbed the palace from the Archbishop of Canterbury). There is the fourteenth-century tithe-barn and the remnants of the college founded in 1395; and this group is the centre of Maidstone's historical interest.

But the High Street has some sound Georgian municipal buildings, the well-mannered Royal Star Hotel, and some agreeably pompous Regency houses as it leaves the town for the sea. Maidstone Gaol has a reputation of enlightenment, and the pictorial interest of having been designed by Daniel Asher Alexander, an architect-engineer of the early nineteenth century. Not so great as Rennie, he was yet concerned with much more than purely structural considerations; his works including the Wapping Docks and, more sinister than Maidstone, Dartmoor Prison; being inspired, since engineers were quite human in those days, by the engravings of Piranesi.

Maidstone has a great cricket history, and the County Week is held on Mote Park's charming ground. It has, too, at a safe distance from the town, a private zoo. Historical celebrities are Hazlitt, the good portrait painter who became a famous essayist; born in

1778 in Earl Street, where his father was minister of the Meeting House; and Anthony Woodville, brother-in-law of Edward IV, whose translation into English of a French translation from the Latin was the first book ever printed in England—by Caxton of Tenterden. Woodville, who became Lord Rivers, was most unfortunately drawn back from literature into politics, and eventually executed by the wicked Richard Crook-back.

At Allington, a very small village by a lock on the Medway, the barges sail past Sir Thomas Wyatt's great Norman Castle, whose vast bastions and moat are immensely pictorial. The site has associations with Britons, Romans, and Saxons, but I am more interested in the Tudor Sir Thomas who brought the sonnet form from Italy. That fruitful poetic convention—some would call it a strait-jacket—flourished in its power of succinct expression until the modern movement exchanged the bonds of prosody for the greater handicap of lawlessness. Sir Thomas had loved Anne Boleyn; his son plotted to oppose Lady Jane Grey to the Spanish ascendency, and died for his failure.

This is a district marked by pre-history, for at Aylesford, the traditional site of the battle between Hengist and Horsa and the Britons, you can see Kit's Coty House. It is a cromlech consisting of three great upright stones crowned by a horizontal ten-tonner; a mysterious monument, presumably sepulchral, marking a hill above the village. Not far off, Addington has the Countless Stones, and Trottiscliffe (pronounced Trosley) the Coldrum.

But Aylesford has lately brought its history up to date, as it were, by receiving back to the Friary that order of Carmelites which was expelled at the Dissolution. This is the first return of a dispossessed order to its old home.

Founded on Mount Carmel in 1155; ejected from Palestine only eighty years later; and encouraged by the Crusaders to settle in Europe; the Carmelites came to England in the thirteenth century, and this, their first friary there, was founded by Richard Grey, Lord of Codnor. Nearly 300 years later it was surrendered to the Bishop of Dover acting for Henry VIII.

On 31 October 1949, 400 years after that, a party of friars, white-cloaked and brown-habited, processed chanting the Litany of the Saints from Aylesford's mediaeval bridge to the Friary. The gatehouse had survived to welcome them—it had received the Royal Commissioners at the time of the eviction; so also had the fine refectory at present serving as a chapel; a fifteenth-century courtyard, and the water-gate leading to the quay. I am sorry to hear that it was Sir Thomas Wyatt the sonneteer who, on being awarded the Friary at the Dissolution, pulled down some of its buildings and all of the old church.

East Malling (Malling rhymes with "falling") has plenty of old cottages and, in the church, the tombs of two men of opposite politics. They may not have been much separated however, by sentiment. Matthew Tomlinson was gaoler, companion on the mortal journey, and almost friend of Charles I; and Sir Thomas Twysden later sat in judgment on the regicides. Of present interest at East Malling is the Agricultural Research station, which brings scientific findings to the fruit-growing industry.

Leybourne is on the other side of the main road, between the two Mallings: a small village where the Norman Castle of the de Leybournes has been converted into a private house; and the little church, originating at the same period, has since been much altered. Architectural history is a little difficult to sort out in this ancient corner.

It is much easier to follow at West Malling, an excellent large village, spacious and unspoiled. The broad street turns sharply by fine Georgian houses to approach the Norman Abbey, which now again is a convent. It has an imposing tower built by Gundulph, Bishop of Rochester; St. Leonard's Tower is his too—probably part of his private fortified house; and West Malling church has another Norman Tower. But I think it is the generous planning and permeating Georgian character of the place which is its chief virtue.

Offham, Comp, and Platt are pleasant villages to the north of Mereworth Woods, but you must keep to the main road for Ightham. This makes it necessary to go through Borough Green, which is probably the ugliest village in Kent, although Dunton Green, beyond Sevenoaks, runs it pretty close. Ightham, on the other hand, is famed for prettiness. There are many romantic half-timbered houses, but some of them are masqueraders and one has beams painted on the plaster. Its position on a main road seems to me to have spoiled the village, giving it a somewhat dolled-up air, and disqualifying it for pottering. The deplorable Sir Charles Sedley is buried in the church. He was probably even more of a Restoration cad than Rochester, since although both were drunks, it is not recorded that Rochester was in the habit of going about the London streets in the nude. Yet Sedley, too, was a lyric poet who addressed himself to Chloris and Celia and wrote "Phyllis is my only joy". I think he too may have found love to be the cordial drop in the nauseous draft of life.

Ightham lies by Oldbury Hill, whose Iron Age earthworks have disclosed much archaeological lore. The expert, Benjamin Harrison, who lived here for many years, discovered as early as 1865 that some of the flint tools of Oldbury were about a million years old.

We are now on the edge of the Ragstone Ridge, and soil is light and sandy. Nutteries are plentiful and so are small orchards, but the wealden sense is missing. Kentish rag gives variety and texture to villages, of which my favourites are Ivy Hatch, Plaxtol, and Shipbourne. The first is tiny, but beautifully arranged, with a pub, a shop, and a handful of old houses; the nearest to the most romantic of all the great houses of Kent—Ightham Mote. Much of this is as old as Pulteney's Penshurst but much more haphazard; expressing with its half-timbered storey over the moat-washed stone the sense of architectural love at first sight; beautiful in texture, and lying in a hole off an unfrequented lane. I find it a little chaotic for my taste; a little ghostly and oppressive; without any hint of brightness and grace. But it is full of charm.

Plaxtol is a little way eastward; approached from Ivy Hatch along a ridge-road giving fine wealden views. The church is mid-seventeenth century, and therefore something of a rarity, but it has suffered some restoration. Much good building in stone, brick, and half-timber collects round the village centre. There is Nut Tree Hall, all beams and plaster, and Old Soar, a mile out, is a National Trust property as old as the late thirteenth century, once a possession of the Culpeppers. It is joined on to a Georgian red brick farmhouse in such a way that two divergent traditions meet harmoniously.

In this strangely remote and even, sometimes, sad stretch of country—its beauty is

Rats Castle, near Plaxtol

guarded and reserved—the little offshoots of the Crayford paper-mills do not seem too obtrusive. You pass them on the way from Dunk's Green up to the edge of Mereworth Woods. Here is Rat's Castle, an old house on an isolated ridge from which you get a wonderful view of the Weald. The sense of remoteness is enhanced by the name.

Fairlawne is a great house between Plaxtol and Shipbourne; easily visible from the road; a product, I should say, of the seventeenth and eighteenth centuries. It was the home of Sir Harry Vane, a Puritan victim of the Restoration. Escaping from persecution at home, he went to America, and was Governor of Massachusetts at the age of twenty-four. But the refugees from religious persecution were themselves disinclined to leave people's consciences free, and Vane came back to England. Although he seems to have been neither regicide nor traitor, he was thought by Charles II too dangerous to be allowed to live.

He is buried in Shipbourne church, which has been infelicitously reconstructed around him in dead Gothic Revival style. But Shipbourne Green is altogether delightful, more like the wealden commons of West Sussex than any I know in Kent. A strange celebrity of this village was the Georgian poet Christopher Smart; the author of the *Song to David*, whose tragic muses were drink and insanity.

I am very fond, too, of Underriver; especially the approach from Ivy Hatch, where Absoloms and Underriver House overlook park-like fields to the Tunbridge Wells ridge. From the village, Carter's Hill takes you up to the woods of Fawke Common and Bitchet Green, showing views as fine as any in Kent; or to Stone Street village in a pleasant clearing and Godden Green between Knole Park and the Wildernesse estate. The latter village just manages to preserve its rural character in face of the overpowering aura of golf and expensive residentialism which pervades the Wildernesse and Seal village.

Another way from Underriver is by confined lanes to the main road at the bottom of River Hill—that testing place for cars and the patience of their drivers. To the west of it is Weald—officially Sevenoaks Weald—where there is a green and a bit of a view and a scattering of cottages. (Kennels and chicken-farms, however, mark it most insistently for me.) Here lived Edward Thomas, poet victim of the first world war, who wrote the little poem which I love: "Yes, I remember Adlestrop". (I would quote it, but I am not in Gloucestershire.) He lent his cottage to W. H. Davies, who, Mr. Church tells us, was delightfully inspired, as he sat writing there one morning, by a butterfly settling on his pencil. It was to Weald, too, that Colonel Lindbergh came after the terrible tragedy of the murder of his child.

The way home for me is up Bayley's Hill or Hubbard's Hill from which, almost all the time, you can turn and stare at the great wooded stretches of the Weald; but I must put off that return and get back to River Hill to approach Sevenoaks. On the Common before you reach the town, there are, indeed, seven oaks; standing near the square and bright "White Hart", but of course vastly younger than Sevenoaks itself. This pub and these trees are the introduction to Knole.

I am tempted to say, simply, go and see Knole if you have not already done so; or buy and read V. Sackville-West's *Knole and the Sackvilles*. It might suggest a seemly humility to say no more than this; but more probably an evasion of the problem. For it certainly is a problem to extract a visual essence from such a mass of historical and artistic details.

One must say, I think, that Knole was built, in the main, by Archbishop Bourchier at the end of the fifteenth century and remained an archiepiscopal palace till Cranmer's time; that it inevitably passed to Henry VIII, and was in royal possession till Elizabeth gave it to her cousin, Thomas Sackville, who married the daughter of "Bloody Baker" of Sissinghurst. Sackville was a writer, statesman, and diplomat upon whom James I conferred the earldom of Dorset, later stepped up to a dukedom. More than two and a quarter centuries later, the dukedom died out and Knole went to a daughter who had married a West. The family names were joined and the family ownership unbroken. The Sackville literary and artistic tradition continues to flourish.

But the vision of Knole? Perhaps the most famous house in England, and certainly one of the biggest, it lies like an Oxford college in a great deer-park full of small hills and great trees. From the road coming into Sevenoaks it looks almost like a compact village composed by a master architect and the skill of weather and time. The Kentish ragstone, seen at that distance, is a soft brownish blurr, but when you get up to the house you find a texture of gentlest beauty; the crisp and tender patina which only centuries of weather can achieve.

Knole is more orderly in design than Penshurst; more beautiful both texturally and architecturally; more magnificently aloof by reason of its isolation from village or town. But I think it is much less friendly. The great hall is cold and, in spite of the exuberance of Jacobean detail, austere; and most of the state-rooms are high-windowed and sombre. (This does not apply to the drawing-room, with its ornate frieze and overpowering Louis XIV gold furniture.) The painted staircase is most ingenious, and so is the wall-painting in the Cartoon Gallery, but—well, I suppose I don't really care for the elaboration of sixteenth-century Italian painters, and prefer the simplicity of Lady Betty Germaine's comparatively small rooms, sombre though they are.

There is an amusing story here. Lady Betty was a relation of the Sackvilles, and adopted one of them, Lord George, on condition that he took her name. In face of so much splendour and renown at Knole, I cannot help being perversely pleased by the tale of Lord George. After the battle of Minden, he was found by court martial to be "unfit to serve His Majesty in any military capacity whatsoever"; yet the War of American Independence found him in the North government as Secretary of State for the Colonies. He seems to have done a good deal to lose that war, since Generals Howe and Burgoyne, who were to have joined forces on the Hudson River, never received their proper orders because Lord George was unwilling to forgo a weekend at Knole. As a result, Burgoyne was forced to surrender at Saratoga. Later, as a member of the cabinet which could deal neither with the American colonies nor with the Gordon Riots, Lord George Germaine was threatened with impeachment by Fox and Burke after the final collapse of the war at Yorktown; but suffered nothing worse than loss of office.

The top or southern end of Sevenoaks High Street is as pleasant a country-town street as you could wish to find. There is the school with its flanking almshouses; the sound and solid Royal Oak Hotel; the little old Post Office; the admirable seventeenth-century Chantry House and the Old Rectory standing one on each side of St. Nicholas' Parish Church; and the Georgian Old House. The entrance to Knole gives no suggestion of the grandeur it introduces, but a glimpse of the park lures you through the gates. On each side of them a few rather badly messed-up Georgian houses back on to the park and face the High Street.

St. Nicholas' is built of excellent weathered ragstone, with a thirteenth-century nave and a fifteenth-century chancel. There is the monument to the Kentish historian William Lambarde, author of the first county history, printed in 1576: *Perambulation of Kent: containing the Description, Hystorie, and Customes of that Shyre.*

William Sevenoke founded the school and almshouses. He is supposed to have been a foundling discovered weeping in a hollow tree; brought up under the name of his village and apprenticed to an ironmonger. He became Lord Mayor of London in 1418 in the progressive interest, and was succeeded by Dick Whittington.

I have seen it written that Sevenoaks School and almshouses were designed by Lord Burlington, but I find it hard to believe that this is true. They are of his century, but in their uncompromising gauntness they have, I fear, few but negative virtues. The central block has been spoiled, apparently not long after its building, by a piece stuck on to ruin its symmetry; detail is crude, and the ragstone here is in one of its grey and doleful moods. I think Burlington and his illustrious collaborator William Kent would have done something more gracious than this.

At the entrance to the shopping area you are at the highest point of the town, about 500 feet up, and can see over a little public garden to the great sequoia in the grounds of

Emmetts at Ide Hill. From many points, too, the Downs near Polhill are visible. Before the High Street and London Road join in a V there is the White House, with a Regency façade sheltering a display of antiques; and the Red House, a fine red brick early eighteenth-century building suitably harbouring a long-established firm of solicitors. London Road slopes dismally down to the station, but the High Street has the "Chequers" in brown and yellow plaster over a mediaeval framework; the rather similar Bligh's Hotel, and a fair number of pleasant upper storeys over the shops.

At the end of it is the very old and honourable Vine cricket ground, where the great Surrey players, Frame and "Shock" White, were wont to face the Hambledon men of old Nyren. Frame was a fast bowler who played for his county in 1749 when he was fifteen; and for England versus Hambledon at Sevenoaks when he was forty. White put up his record score of 197 on the Vine. Such deeds are sometimes celebrated there now, when the players appear in traditional top-hats, wielding bats of improbable contour.

From the Vine, Sevenoaks falls rather obviously into suburban development to Otford, Seal, and Riverhead. But the latter village, skirting Montreal Park, has some fine Georgian houses on the Sundridge road, and an early Gothic Revival church by the great classicist Decimus Burton. You can branch off in the village square to Chipstead, a sweetly winding and confined village surrounded by some unfortunate speculative building; or carry on straight down the westerly road to Bessel's Green. It is pleasantly composed, with a range of old houses to the west and a long terrace of early nineteenth-century cottages which would be charming if only they were painted. The houses on the main road, opposite the green, are mostly "good class" speculation, but there are a few little bits of Regency or Early Victorian romantic on the edge of the Chipstead Park estate.

Beyond the Darent and the little branch railway-line the whiff of suburbia dies away into the country air, dispelled by the territories of Chevening and Morant's Court. A little dead-end road with a few cottages and an old church—that is all there is of Chevening hamlet, behind which the great house lies at the foot of the Downs. The Pilgrims' Road has disappeared here after skirting Hogtrough and Sundridge Hill sloping sharply up to Knockholt.

As you stand in the entrance court of Chevening looking north, you are at once astonished by a brilliant white rectangle against the trees on the Downland horizon. At first sight it appears to be solid, an obelisk or monolith of some sort; but in fact it is void—a meticulous cutting in the trees exactly on the main axis of the great house. The "Keyhole", as it is known, appears on old drawings of the estate, and its accurate setting out over the undulations of the park must have involved some quite complicated surveying. The same idea is beautifully carried out beyond the great lawns south of the house, where vast cavernous drives have been cut in the woods at various angles. None shows the sky, and they must be delightfully contemplative for evening wanderings; romantic in conception, but classic in form. The great lake is in the same spirit, and all the garden and grounds have just enough formality for grandeur and picturesqueness for warmth.

Chevening was almost certainly designed by Inigo Jones, but nobody would be likely to guess this from its present aspect. Old drawings show a square red brick house with pitched roof, dormers, and balustrade—very typical of the seventeenth century. It belonged to the Lennard family till, early in the eighteenth century, it was bought by James Stanhope, Prime Minister in all but name (the office was not so designated until it was held a little later by Sir Robert Walpole). As a military commander he captured Port Mahon in the Balearics, and when created an Earl he took the Viscounty of Mahon as his second title. Architecturally he did well by the house, adding the stable and library blocks which flank the main building and form the forecourt, and linking the composition with curving galleries.

The third Earl was a very notable scientist and inventor; known, for his radical tendencies, as "Citizen Stanhope"; father of the famous and eccentric Lady Hester; and brother-in-law of William Pitt. It may have been his scientific knowledge which persuaded him to dispense with an architect—although in those days science and art were much closer than they are now. Anyway, about 1790 he unfortunately covered the main block of Chevening with yellow mathematical tiles, which, clamped on to the old brickwork, are almost impossible to remove without much damage and expense. This treatment extended to a high parapet wall which did away with the dormers and made the roof invisible. The elevations could, of course, have been successfully brought up to date by a skilled architect, but I am afraid that the third Lord Stanhope spoiled Chevening, and that it is now neither Inigo Jones nor, very convincingly, late Georgian. But I think that the entrance front, where the tiles have darkened between the applied pilasters, is decidedly imposing for all that: a grey eminence flanked by rosy wings.

Inside, the most interesting elements are the dining-room, panelled with a Jonesian décor; the great tapestry room whose magnificent hangings were given to the first Lord Stanhope, as a reward for Port Mahon, by Frederick I of Prussia; and the same Stanhope's library, with his fine collection of books as he had them. There are many pictures of Stanhopes and Pitts by famous artists, and original manuscripts or letters by Marlborough, Byron, and Kipling among others.

During the air-raids of 1940, about twenty bombs fell on or around Chevening, of which one at least went right through the house. But not one exploded, and it may be that the great house owes its survival to the work of Czech saboteurs.

I suppose that the greater part of the Battle of Britain was fought in Kentish skies; and probably, too, the V.I. campaign was most hotly waged there. No part of the county was restful in those days, but I associate the Darent valley and the Downs behind it more closely with the aerial onslaught than any other part of Kent. Biggin Hill air-station is on the westernmost range of the Kentish Downs, and it is hard to believe that any other played a greater part in the battle. It was here that the massed German formations were broken up and shot down or chased away; and the countryside probably accepted a greater share of bombs and invaders falling from the sky than any place except individual target areas.

Sundridge is cut in two by the main road, and has been extended haphazardly along it; but the Square has a pleasant early nineteenth-century character and the village is rich in domestic architecture: the Old Rectory, the Manor House, Sundridge Place, the Red House and the White; all of them a little way up the hill from the Square; and, on the main road, Bishop's Cottage, and the Old Hall of fifteenth-century half-timbering.

On the other side of the main road, Combe Bank is a big Georgian house of rather discouraging mien. Lord Ferrers was the last peer executed in England—for killing his steward in 1760. He was tried in Westminster Hall and hanged at Tyburn. Long afterwards, his aged widow was burnt to death at Combe Bank. Another occupant was the boy who was later famous as Cardinal Manning—he would be pleased to know that the house is now a convent school of the ancient faith.

Sundridge church is old and stout and nicely sited on a rise above the Old Rectory—on still evenings I can hear its bells from my home. It has the grave of Anne Seymour Damer the sculptress; who was so much of a Bonapartist that she sent Napoleon her wishes for his success on the eve of Waterloo—in those days quislings were treated with remarkable leniency. Oddly enough, she was taught her art by Carrachi, the Corsican who was eventually executed for trying to assassinate Napoleon. A relation of Horace Walpole, she inherited Strawberry Hill on his death.

Only the estates of Combe Bank and Brasted Place serve to separate Sundridge from Brasted, as the Darent flows through narrow banks to Westerham. Brasted Place epitomises, even more than the architectural grace of our Augustan days, the ruthless vandalism of the Victorians. For in this peaceful park Robert Adam designed what was then considered a modest villa for Dr. Turton, court physician to George III. It is said that the modesty was stipulated by the doctor in order to forestall any possible expensive visit by the Monarch. Be that as it may, Brasted Place is a piece of grandiose simplicity by the Scottish master; gracious, serene, dignified. But when some Victorian owner decided to build on to it, he proceeded with gusto to jam on a monstrous structure in the style of—one might as well say "French Château" as anything else.

From Brasted Place, Charles Louis Napoleon Bonaparte made his way to Boulogne to attempt the throne of France. That was in 1840, when he was well known in Brasted; eight years before the Revolution which made him deputy for Paris as, of all things, a nominee of the working classes. After his reactionary and absurd exercise of Imperial power and his defeat by the Prussians on whom he had declared war in 1870, he returned to Kent—this time to Chislehurst.

Brasted High Street is spacious and consistently well-mannered architecturally. Its historical status, I think, was raised much above the dubious fame of Napoleon III by the pilots from Biggin Hill whose favourite place of relaxation in the decisive days of 1940 was the "White Hart". Here, on the black-out board at the entrance to the bar, they signed their names in chalk. The war over, the board was taken down, framed, and officially unveiled in the bar where so many young celebrities had enjoyed intervals of pleasure and comparative safety. And you can read the names now: "Sailor" Malan, Brian Kingcome, and Tony Bartley, who survived the ordeal; "Screwball" Beurling, who died on another mission; and many others who saved us.

Westerham is almost on the Surrey boundary—a nice large village or small town where the sculpture of General Wolfe dominates the sloping triangular green. He lived at Quebec House, a National Trust property of beautiful brickwork; was born at the Vicarage, and stayed at the "George and Dragon". He is, therefore, the essential man of Westerham.

Squerryes, a beautiful house of the late seventeenth or early eighteenth century, has the source of the Darent; and by it is a little road which takes you to the top of the

Westerham Village

Ragstone Ridge at Crockham Hill. In the church, Octavia Hill, one of the founders of the National Trust, is buried; this and a rather formless grouping of houses and cottages have a magnificent view over the Weald of Kent. There is, too, lying above the territory known as Puddledock, Winston Churchill's "Chartwell". Like the house of Wolfe, an earlier British hero, Mr. Churchill's home is a National Trust property; but he still lives there to enjoy its enviable site overlooking the vast wealden acres. I should say that "Chartwell" was originally a smallish seventeenth-century house; and that it has fairly lately been enlarged by an ingenious architect not too clever over his choice of bricks.

Between "Chartwell" and Toys Hill, you lose the view in deep lanes till, rounding a bend by Bardogs Farm, you climb the hill which gives it back to you more lovely than ever. Toys Hill and Ide Hill are both "beauty spots" guarded by National Trust land; but I think the best prospect from all this great range of hills is got from the Tally Ho Inn at Toys Hill. The thick layers of woods roll away to the south to be topped in the

Kentish ricks

distance by the crest of Ashdown Forest; and to the east you see the sharply rising foreground which ends in the finger of Ide Hill church. You can pick out the orchards and oasts of Henden, and the farmlands of Winkhurst and Wickhurst, while from the ridge lane above Bardogs westerly views carry the eye far into Surrey and Sussex.

Toys Hill is a pretty little collection of not very distinguished cottages, and it lacks a church to give it an architectural centre; but the village hall puts an inhabitant of Ide Hill to some shame, and visitors are not, like him, constantly thwarted for views by the lie of the land.

The steep hill runs north by National Trust lands to its summit; and down again to Brasted Chart, a long string-out of houses, cottages, post office, and pub, which cannot properly be called a village. My favourite walk is from Ide Hill's "Emmetts" to the "Tally Ho" and back by way of Scord's Farm and the footpath through fields and woods; to come into Ide Hill village by the school. I don't suppose that many people in our village know that the school was designed by the extremely distinguished but unutterably boring Victorian architect, George Edmund Street. Compared with his more famous building, the London Law Courts, this little work has a cheerful mien, and many worse things have been done for education since his time; but for me Street, who is in process of being revived by our neo-Victorian critics, is very dead indeed.

We have a green sloping up to our Gothic Revival church, which, horrible on close scrutiny—I wish I could pin it on Street—is very effective silhouetted on top of the hill 700 feet up. Behind it, the Old Vicarage has surely one of the loveliest sites in the south of England; an old garden with great beeches framing the superb and distant view. (Sometimes, seen from here, from the Trust ground, or from the village hall, it looks like a seascape; when mist lies in the valley and Crowborough Beacon rises like a beckoning island above.)

I must admit that we haven't much in the way of architectural beauty. The Old

Vicarage is rather nondescript in ragstone and brick mostly of the early nineteenth century; Ide Cottage is older, part of a pleasant little weatherboarded group on the green; the Cock Inn is probably sixteenth to seventeenth century, an altogether admirable little pub; and Rosemary Cottage is early Georgian. Some of the later cottages near the general stores have a decent simplicity, but there is too much slate roofing for a truly Kentish aspect; and Ide Hill's offshoot of Goathurst Common is a raffish and almost sinister collection of old and new cottages and shacks and shanties till building fades out by the "Woodman", Back Lane, and Whitley Forest.

We have a tradition of gypsy encampments and of escapes from the law; the old name, delightfully, was Idle Hill; and it is obvious that only 150 years ago this was a very remote and minute settlement. It still has the air of a place without a long history and I am not sure where it gets its speech: "dane the tane" for "down the town", and "somewhen". I don't think this is generally Kentish, although H. G. Wells on occasion used the pleasant "somewhen".

Ruminating on this and that—that Wells was a greater man than Shaw because he took life seriously; that architecture was once an art; that Kent has the loveliest and most unspoiled landscape less than thirty miles from London; and that I have finished, for the time being, my explorations in search of a vision—I walk a little way down the hill, past the cricket-ground where sixes are cheap, and into my home opposite. I cannot see the views over the Weald ,but I can hear the sound of the bat and ball.

Houses at Tonbridge

RIV. THAMES
SHEERNESS
QUEENBOROUGH
ISLE OF SHEPPEY
Elmley Island
Elmley
Eastchurch
Minster
RIVER MEDWAY
Blyth Sands
Thames Haven
St. Mary's Marshes
Cooling Marshes
Halstow Marshes
Allhallows
Grain
Wallend
Port Victoria
Stoke Saltings
Stoke
Cliffe
Cooling
High Halstow
St. Mary's Hoo
Hoo
Higham
Chetney Marshes
Wireless Tel. Sta.
GRAVESEND
NORTHFLEET
TILBURY
East Tilbury
West Tilbury
Chadwell St. Mary
Little Thurrock
GRAYS THURROCK
W. Thurrock
Purfleet
Stifford
Aveley
Wennington
Belvedere
Abbey Wood
WOOLWICH
ERITH
East Wickham
Bexley Heath
Welling
Eltham
Crayford
DARTFORD
Stone
Greenhithe
Swanscombe
BEXLEY
Sidcup
Wilmington
North Cray
Foots Cray
CHISLEHURST
St. Paul's Cray
St. Mary Cray
Orpington
Bromley Common
Farnborough
Chelsfield
Downe
Cudham
Halstead
Knockholt
Chevening
Dunton Green
Riverhead
Chipstead
Brasted
Sundridge
SEVENOAKS
Sevenoaks Weald
Knole
Ivy Hatch
Shipbourne
Hildenborough
Leigh
TONBRIDGE
SOUTHBOROUGH
Speldhurst
Bidborough
Penshurst
Chiddingstone
Hever
EDENBRIDGE
R. Eden
Cowden
Pembury
Southfleet
Darenth
Sutton at Hone
South Darenth
Horton Kirby
Swanley Junction
Crockenhill
Farningham
Eynsford
Lullingstone
Shoreham
Otford
Kemsing
Seal
Ightham
WROTHAM
Wrotham Heath
Borough Green
Platt
Offham
Trottiscliffe
Addington
Ryarsh
Birling
Snodland
Kingsdown
Stansted
Ash
Ridley
Hartley
Fawkham
Longfield
Singlewell
Shorne
Chalk
Chequers Street
Cobham
Nurstead
Meopham
Luddesdown
Cuxton
Halling
Wouldham
Strood
Frindsbury
ROCHESTER
CHATHAM
GILLINGHAM
Upchurch
Iwade
Lower Halstow
Luton
Rainham
Newington
Borstal
Capstone
Burham
Kit's Coty
Eccles
New Hythe
Aylesford
Boxley
Detling
Bredhurst
Lidsing
Stockbury
Hartlip
Bicknor
Hucking
Bredgar
Milsted
Kingsdown
Wormshill
Doddington
Newnham
MILTON REGIS
SITTINGBOURNE
Tunstall
Bapchild
Rodmersham
Lynsted
Murston
Tonge
Greenstreet
Woodstock
Frinsted
Eastling
Wichling
Otterden
Throwley
Stalisfield Green
Warren Street
Lenham
Lenham Heath
Charing
Charing Heath
Westwell
Leacon
Egerton
Boughton Malherbe
Ulcombe
Little Chart
Pluckley
Surrenden Dering
The Forstal
Hothfield
Dowle Street
Pluckley Sta.
Smarden
Biddenden Green
Headcorn
Frittenden
Southernden
Staplehurst
Marden
Harrietsham
Hollingbourne
Eyhorne Street
Broomfield
Leeds Castle
Kings Wood
Sutton Valence
East Sutton
Chart Sutton
Boughton Monchelsea
Langley
Linton
Loose
Otham
Bearsted
Thornham
Vinters
The Mote
Tovil
MAIDSTONE
R. Len
Allington
Ditton
Beybourne
Leybourne
East Malling
WEST MALLING
Larkfield
Barming
East Barming
Teston
Wateringbury
Mereworth
Claygate Cross
Plaxtol
Dunk's Green
West Peckham
Oxen Hoath
Nettlestead
Nettlestead Green
Farleigh
Yalding
Hunton
Laddingford
Mockbeggar
Hale Street
Hadlow
East Peckham
Golden Green
Riv. Medway
Whetsted
Tudeley
Capel
Paddock Wood
Collier Street
River Teise
Brenchley
Horsmonden
Matfield
Riv. Beult
Mitbush
N O R T H D O W N S
K E N T
Watling Street
Pilgrims Way
Roman Road

Forest Row
Hartfield
Withyham
Eridge Cas.
Frant
Abbey
Lamberhurst
Scotney Castle
Kilndown
CRANBROOK
Hartley
Bedgebury
St. Michaels
Woodchurch
TENTERDEN
Benenden
Hole Park
Rolvenden Sta.
Leigh Green
Brook Street
Kenardington
Coleman's Hatch
Fisher's Gate
Friar's Gate
Boarshead
Cousley Wood
Wadhurst
Threeleg Cross
Flimwell
Hawkhurst Sta.
Iden Green
Rolvenden
Highgate
Reading Street
Small Hythe
Rolvenden Layne
Crowborough
Mark Cross
Tidebrook
Ticehurst
Hawkhurst
The Moor
Rotherfield
Sandhurst
Wittersham Road Sta.
Appledore
ISLE OF OXNEY
Stone
Wittersham
Newenden
Nutley
Stonegate
Ticehurst Rd. Sta.
Hurst Green
High Hurstwood
Mayfield
Witherenden Hill
Etchingham
Bodiam
R. Rother
Fairfield
Brookland
Cowden
Five Ashes
Broadhurst
Burwash
R. Dudwell
Willard's Hill
Salehurst
Ewhurst
Junction Rd. Halt
Northiam
Four Oaks
Maresfield
Fletching
Hadlow Down
Robertsbridge
Beckley
Iden
Rother Levels
Buxted
Burwash Common
Staple Cross
Reasmarsh
UCKFIELD
Heathfield
Broadoak
Ozley's Green
Brightling
Playden
East Guldeford
East Guldeford Level
Framfield
Possingworth
Little London
Punnett's Town
Mountfield
Vinehall Street
Broad Oak
R. Tillingham
RYE
Rye Harbour
Waldron
Dallington
Rushlake Green
Netherfield
Whatlington
Sedlescombe
Brede
Udimore
Camber Castle
Little Horsted
Warbleton
Horam
Penhurst
R. Brede
WINCHELSEA
Rye Bay
R. Ouse
Isfield
Halland
East Hoathly
Ponts Green
BATTLE
Abbey 1066
Westfield
Icklesham
Pett Level
Barcombe Mills
Shortgate
Chiddingly
Poul Mile
Cowbeech
Bodlestreet Green
Ashburnham Place
Catsfield
Beauport Park
Guestling
Pett
Laughton
Whitesmith
Gardner Street
Ninfield
Crowhurst
Gt. Ridge
Cliff End
Ringmer
Hellingly
Hellingly Hosp.
Horsebridge
Magham Down
Herstmonceux
Boreham Street
Hollington
Ore
Fairlight
Cliffe Hill
Glyndebourne
LEWES
Upper Dicker
Ripe
HAILSHAM
Warting
Wallers Haven
Hooe
Sidley Green
HASTINGS
St. Leonards
Glynde
Chalvington
Priory
PEVENSEY LEVELS
Little Common
BEXHILL
Beddingham
Selmeston
Berwick Sta.
Arlington
West Firle
Firle Beacon 718
Alciston
Berwick
Polegate
Wilmington
Hankham
Pevensey
Westham
Pevensey Bay
Tarring Neville
South Heighton
Denton
Alfriston
Lullington
Folkington
Willingdon
Hampden Park
Langney Point
Litlington
Jevington
Bishopstone
Willingdon Hill
East Blatchington
Westdean
SEAFORD
EASTBOURNE
Friston
Eastdean
Cuckmere Haven
ASHDOWN FOREST
WEALD
EAST SUSSEX
DOWNS

Foreness Point
MARGATE
WESTGATE ON SEA
White Ness
NORTH FOR
Wireless Tel.
Leysdown
HERNE BAY
Reculver
Hillborough
Birchington
ISLE OF THANET
BROADSTAIRS
Shell Ness
Swalecliffe
St. Nicholas at Wade
Acol
WHITSTABLE
Whitstable Bay
Haine
Herne
Marshside
Sarre
Monkton
St. Lawrence
RAMSGATE
Seasalter
Chislet
Minster
Hoath
Pegwell Bay
Graveney
Grove Ferry
W. Stourmouth
Bargate
E. Stourmouth
Honey Hill
Grove
Westmarsh
Goodnestone
Broadoak
Tylerhill
Westbere
Stodmarsh
Preston
Sandwich Flats
Hernhill
Blean
Sturry
Great Stour
Elmstone
Richborough
Fordwich
Hoaden
Boughton Street
Wickhambreux
Ash
Dunkirk
CANTERBURY
Ickham
SANDWICH
Mental Hospl.
Marshborough
Brake Lightship
Harbledown
Wingham
THE SMALL DOWNS
Selling
Oversland
Chartham Hatch
Littlebourne
Woodnesborough
Thanington
Staple
Worth
Old Wives Lees
Milton
Bekesbourne
Nackington
Patrixbourne
Goodnestone
Eastry
Shottenden
Chartham
Bridge
Chillenden
Ham
Adisham
Knowlton
Tilmanstone
Chilham
Aylesham
Lower Hardres
Bishopsbourne
Nonington
Sholden
DEAL
Molash
Petham
Easole Street
Betteshanger
Northbourne
THE DOWNS
Godmersham
Kingston
Great Mongeham
Upper Hardres
Womenswold
WALMER
Barham
Barfreston
Ripple
Solestreet
Crundale
Bossingham
Derringstone
Wollage Green
Eythorne
Sutton
Boughton Aluph
Waltham
Olantigh Towers
Broome Park
Waldershare
Kingsdown
Ringwould
Stelling
Shepherdswell
Coldred
WYE
Stelling Minnis
West Langdon
Martin Mill Sta.
Denton
Wootton
Whitfield
East Langdon
Hastingleigh
St. Margaret's at Cliffe
West Cliffe
Elmsted
Lydden
Temple Ewell
Guston
Brook
South Foreland Lights
Elham
Swingfield
St. Margaret's Bay
Mily. School
Hinxhill
Acrise
River
Buckland
SOUTH FORELAND
Brabourne
Ottinge
Swingfield Minnis
Alkham
Willesborough
Stowting
Ferry to Calais
St. Radigund's Abbey
Priory Sta.
DOVER
Lyminge
Hawkinge
Monks Horton
Paddlesworth
Citadel
Smeeth
Horton Park
Capel le Ferne
Hougham
Mersham
Postling
Sellindge
Stanford
Beachborough
East Wear Bay
Newington
Aldington
Saltwood
Shorncliffe Camp
FOLKESTONE
Wireless Tel. Sta.
Bonnington
Lympne
W. Hythe
SANDGATE
Bilsington
Canal
HYTHE
Burmarsh
Dymchurch Redoubt
Newchurch
Dymchurch
St. Mary in the Marsh
Littlestone on Sea Sta.
Littlestone on Sea
NEW ROMNEY
Romney Sands
East Road
Greatstone on Sea
LYDD
Varne Lightship
Denge Marsh
Denge Beach
DUNGENESS
STRAIT OF D

Index

References to illustrations are not included in the Index